Richard Wright

with a new foreword
Arnold Rampersad

The Northeastern
Library of
Black Literature
edited by
Richard Yarborough

LAWD TODAY

LAWD TODAY

Other titles in
The Northeastern Library of Black Literature
edited by Richard Yarborough

WILLIAM DEMBY
The Catacombs

W. E. B. DU BOIS
The Quest of the Silver Fleece

JESSIE REDMON FAUSET
There Is Confusion

GAYL JONES
White Rat

JULIAN MAYFIELD
The Hit and *The Long Night*

CLAUDE MCKAY
Home to Harlem

ALBERT MURRAY
Train Whistle Guitar

J. SAUNDERS REDDING
Stranger and Alone

GEORGE S. SCHUYLER
Black Empire
Black No More

WALLACE THURMAN
Infants of the Spring

Lawd Today

RICHARD WRIGHT

with a new foreword by Arnold Rampersad

NORTHEASTERN UNIVERSITY PRESS
Boston

Library of Congress Cataloging in Publication Data
Wright, Richard, 1908–1960.
Lawd today.
I. Title.
PS3545.R815L3   1986   813'.52   86-12840
ISBN 0-930350-99-5 (pbk.)

Printed and bound by Edwards
Brothers, Ann Arbor, Michigan. The
paper is Glatfelter Offset, an acid-free sheet.

MANUFACTURED IN THE UNITED STATES OF AMERICA
94 93 92   6 5 4 3

Ach

CONTENTS

FOREWORD
1

Part One:
COMMONPLACE
7

Part Two:
SQUIRREL CAGE
99

Part Three:
RATS' ALLEY
163

FOREWORD

Posthumously offered literature, especially from an author who published steadily in his or her lifetime, is often inferior work. However, *Lawd Today*, which first appeared in 1963, three years after Richard Wright's untimely death at the age of fifty-two, cannot with justification be called second-rate among his works. While it is certainly flawed, the tale is also quite possibly the second most important novel written by Wright, and it is clearly inferior only to the landmark *Native Son* (1940) among his novels. Far less grand in theme than *The Outsider* (1953), it is also less bleak and didactic than that existentialist story. Certainly it is more compelling than *Savage Holiday* (1954), Wright's somewhat thin and improbable accounting, according to a Freudian scheme, of a lonely white man (there are no blacks in the novel) driven to psychopathic murder. And although conspicuously less rich in characterization and plot, at least in a conventional sense, than *The Long Dream* (1957), *Lawd Today* is nevertheless a more exuberant and spontaneous, as well as a more decisively motivated, piece of fiction than the last novel published in Wright's lifetime.

Lawd Today is a young writer's book, one in which might be seen, sometimes in forms not entirely digested, not only the literary influences that instructed Wright in his fledgling enterprise in fiction but also some of the basic impulses that led him to begin his distinguished career as a writer. Wright started the novel, first called *Cesspool,* sometime around 1934, or about seven years after he arrived in Chicago from his native South at the age of nineteen. Near the end of his time in the South, as he relates with harrowing power in his autobiography, *Black Boy* (1945), Wright had discovered from the charged pages of H. L. Mencken that it was possible for a powerless man to use "words as weapons," and that voluminous reading and steady writing, in the face of all opposition or other discouragement, was the most effective counter to both his own profound sense of isolation and the dismal education he had received as a boy in Mississippi and Arkansas. Not long after his arrival in Chicago, he found in the leftist community there—and especially in the local chapter of the radical John Reed Club (in which he served for some time as executive secretary)—a congenial circle of younger, committed artists who shared his sense of deter-

1

mination that words honed and tempered into radical art could indeed make a difference in life.

Overhauled at least once by 1936, the novel made the rounds of the major commercial publishers without success or encouragement, until at last it disappeared into Wright's files not to surface publicly until after his death. Undeterred by this rejection, however, Wright continued to publish, mainly poetry (in journals such as *New Masses, International Literature,* and *Partisan Review*) and radical journalism (in places such as the Communist *Daily Worker*); but he soon emerged most impressively on the national scene in 1938 as a short story writer with *Uncle Tom's Children: four novellas,* which effectively launched his mature career. Two years later, *Native Son* crowned it.

Why was *Lawd Today* rejected by publishers in the late thirties? The most consistent complaint from them apparently concerned its lack of broad, deep characterization and its skimpiness of plot. Quite possibly, however, editors were repulsed by the extreme realism in the novel, as suggested by its initial title. Although it does not contain passages that actually depict sexual intercourse, the novel is saturated with the language and situations of lust, as it records in accumulating details Wright's sense of the rough-and-ready sexual obsession of its four main characters, Jake Jackson and his friends Bob, Al, and Slim. This obsession, unrelieved by the slightest romantic element, is recounted in langauge and scenes of a frankness and even crudeness seldom seen previously in American literature. In addition, Wright did not conceal the fact that white women were often the objects of fantasies and desires on the part of some black men. White editors might have believed, not without reason, that the American reading public was not ready for such renegade thoughts and undisciplined language on the part of blacks.

For all its rawness, however, *Lawd Today* reveals unmistakably that Wright was already a conscious artist in its composition, and one alert to the functioning of tradition. Perhaps his most significant single debt is to James Joyce, in that the action of the novel takes place roughly in twenty-four hours (mostly on Lincoln's Birthday), as in *Ulysses*; also, the climactic visit to Rose's saloon is reminiscent of a setting of similar importance in Joyce's most famous work. From Henry James, whose prefaces and other essays on fiction Wright had taken to heart, came probably the relentness concern in *Lawd Today* with strictness of point-of-view; we see the action of the book mainly as the "hero" Jake Jackson envisions it, from his awak-

2

ening at eight o'clock one morning to his descent into bloody unconsciousness near dawn the following day.

Important, too, is Wright's sense of kinship with the major American realists and naturalists, themselves descended in some respects from Emile Zola. Not least of all, in its unpolished vigor and vitality, *Lawd Today* reminds one almost inevitably of Stephen Crane's *Maggie: A Girl of the Streets* and Frank Norris's tale of greed, *McTeague*. Certainly Theodore Dreiser's influence is discernible, although the link between *Native Son* and *An American Tragedy* would be a more indelible token of Wright's lasting debt to Dreiser. From James Farrell, author of the *Studs Lonigan* trilogy, with whom Wright discussed at length the art of fiction, he frankly borrowed a number of devices and techniques for *Lawd Today*, including the precise charting of the game of bridge played in the novel (like the football game described in Farrell's *Judgment Day*) and the highlighting of dreams as a guide to the largely unconscious interests and motives of Jake Jackson. From John Dos Passos, whose *U.S.A.* trilogy Wright esteemed highly, came the graphic use of newspaper headlines and radio announcements on which *Lawd Today* depends fairly heavily for a sense both of history and of immediacy.

Lastly, epigraphs taken from the work of Van Wyck Brooks (*America's Coming of Age*), Waldo Frank (*Our America*), and T. S. Eliot (*The Waste Land*) and cited before each of the three sections of the novel indicate, along with his bows to James Joyce and Henry James, that Wright's reading and his ambitions as a writer of fiction had already taken him beyond the scope of realists and naturalists such as Dreiser, Farrell, and Dos Passos. In a real sense, these epigraphs anticipate the modernist philosophical drive that would sweep him beyond his early concerns with the matters of race and radical socialism; that drive would result most pointedly almost twenty years later in the publication of *The Outsider*.

For all these literary influences, however, *Lawd Today* sprang first and foremost out of Wright's life and his particular experiences as a sensitive, highly intelligent black migrant hungry for a sense of achievement and trying to make his way, in the midst of the Depression, in the black South Side of Chicago. What Jake Jackson encounters in his wanderings through the city in *Lawd Today* is essentially what Richard Wright knew on a daily basis either from personal involvement or from distanced but keen observation in Chicago. For example, like Jake Jackson and his three main friends, Wright had worked for some time in the postal service, and thus was able to describe the facilities and the regimen at the Central Post Office with deadly accuracy. "Doc" Higgins, the scheming proprietor of a barbershop and a part-time Republican Party ward boss in the novel, is not unlike the shrewd barbershop proprietor and Republican precinct captain for whom Wright himself had worked. The graphic descriptions of the hold of religion on Jake's wife, Lil, and on broad sections of the black community came no doubt from the generally oppressive place of fundamentalist religion in Wright's own family, as he saw it. Gambling, so prominent a feature of *Lawd Today*, was virtually the chief pastime of the South Side that Wright knew. The black nationalist personalities and their ventures, the confidence men who prey on the gullible, the pimps and prostitutes who fall naturally into place as a part of the landscape of *Lawd Today*—all were at hand, about the author, when *Cesspool* was conceived and revised into *Lawd Today*.

Because so much of the book is rooted in Wright's restless observation of the life about him, *Lawd Today* goes beyond mere literary influence to reveal the first distinct outlines of what would be recognized as his authentic fictional vision. That vision was formed and articulated in the face of ideological and other distractions that often ran counter to it. Although Wright was a member of the Communist Party when the novel was written, it is hard to imagine that the party censors who found *Native Son* hard to swallow would have sanctioned the earlier work. *Lawd Today* reveals Wright in his classic position as an artist and an intellectual: he was uncompromising and fiercely courageous in his moral and social criticism. Faced with social conditions that he found fundamentally intolerable, he did not hesitate to draw unflattering portraits wherever he found them appropriate. As a result, this novel is dramatically pessimistic.

Certainly it is pessimistic where the black masses are concerned. Apart from fleeting pictures of a black communist sympathizer, a bourgeois post office official who scorns Jake, and the lonely figure of a boy reading in a window at one point in the book (to Jake's bewilderment at such a waste of time), virtually all the black characters are seen as leading desperate, even demeaning lives. Wright's sense of discomfort with his community, which is to say his race, ran deep. The palms of Jake Jackson's hands are not dark but "dingy," an unfortunate term to which Wright would revert again in *Black Boy* to describe blacks. Here, as elsewhere in his work, black women seem

4

to bear the brunt of his criticism. The masses, male or female, suggest no potential for redemption, much less revolution; instead, they are seen as creatures dominated variously by lust, avarice, sloth, superstition, and a fatal weakness for violence. If any grand visitation is at hand, it is very possibly an apocalypse—with Jake Jackson and his three friends (one is passionate about the army, another is a consumptive, and the third suffers from a venereal disease) as the four horsemen of war, disease, famine, and death. Because of such unequivocal criticism, *Lawd Today*, like *Native Son,* is a perfect companion piece to Wright's famous catalogue in *Black Boy* of the inadequacies of the culture into which he was born. "Lawd, I wish I was dead," Jake's battered wife, Lil, moans in the last words spoken in the novel. The last lines of *Lawd Today* are as bleak: "Outside an icy wind swept around the corner of the building, whining and moaning like an idiot in a deep black pit."

The main factor that prevents *Lawd Today* from being thoroughly nihilistic raises provocative questions in itself. That factor is the superior quality of life among whites, who are seen only dimly and obliquely in *Lawd Today*, but are made to look fairly attractive in that light. When a group of about fifteen black women troops through the post office, they are portrayed as "round-shouldered and dumpy-looking." In the trail of a group of white women, however, Jake hears "murmurs of laughter, light, silvery." Where the four friends perform their post office duties indifferently at best, then rush to play cards or waste their money on food, drink, and sex, the white workers are seen as generally industrious and purposeful; often they are concerned with getting an education. Behind this distinction is Wright's sense, articulated in *Black Boy* and elsewhere, of the difference between a culture and civilization, with blacks having historically been denied the means to convert the former, which admits of few virtues, into the glorious latter. It might be said with great accuracy that the main purpose of all of Wright's restless, encyclopedic reading and constant writing was to raise himself, and those who would heed him, out the shallows of what he called a culture and toward the humanist heights of civilization.

To some extent, however, *Lawd Today* is premature on this question, in that Wright does not directly connect the lives of American blacks to the lives of American whites—as he would do with historic impact in *Native Son.* And yet there is clear evidence that Wright was moving toward this connection. The principal interplay between the two races comes with the impact of the radio program about the nobility of the life of Abraham Lincoln, which is heard intermittently but loudly throughout most of the novel. In one sense, the interplay emphasizes the failure of Lincoln's act of emancipation and seems to hold the descendants of the slaves accountable. But the bombastic language of the program, contrasting with the illiteracies of the main characters and the terseness of the narrative line, also tells us that Wright is aware of the hollowness of the national myth of freedom and the master race's manipulation of the retelling of history to suit its own ends.

On the other hand, because the white world is barely mentioned, relatively speaking, in *Lawd Today*, the pessimism with which Wright views the black community takes on something of a cosmic significance, as underscored in the closing words of the novel. Against this pessimism is arrayed the ignorant struggle of Jake and his friends to find pleasure, if not meaning, in life. Their often frantic struggle leads to perhaps the chief appeal of *Lawd Today*—its mixture of a sense of purposelessness and hopelessness in life, on one hand, and an almost animal vitality on the other. Not the least attractive feature of this vitality is its comedy; Wright possessed a genuine gift for farce which he seldom indulged in his later works but made a prominent part of *Lawd Today*. His pessimism predominates but is also almost matched by his wonder at the prodigious capacity of his subjects to eat, laugh, and "love." Wonder does not, however, turn to admiration or envy. Wright remains the epitome of the thinking, judging man, firm in his disapproval of what he so graphically describes.

The result is a novel almost always compelling, almost always challenging, and a worthy example of the art by which Richard Wright revolutionized not only the fictional depiction of blacks in the United States but also the American sense of identity where race is concerned.

ARNOLD RAMPERSAD

Part One:

COMMONPLACE

. . . a vast Sargasso Sea—a prodigious welter of unconscious life, swept by groundswells of half-conscious emotion. . . .

Van Wyck Brooks' *America's Coming-of-Age*

Ladies and Gentlemen, Jack Bassett speaking! Station WGN, Tribune Square, Chicago. At the next tonebeat the time will be exactly eight o'clock, Central Standard Time . . . ting! . . . courtesy the Neverstop Watch Company, Ladies and Gentlemen!

Look out of your window! What do you see flapping so proudly and sedately at every corner and over every building entrance? Doesn't it make your heart skip a beat to see Old Glory floating there so beautifully in the morning breeze?

My Dear Friends, our flag is flying high today in honor of one of our greatest Americans, a man who saved his country and bestowed the blessings of liberty and freedom upon millions of his fellowmen!

This is February twelfth, Abraham Lincoln's Birthday!

At this time Professor Weatherspoon, Head of the Department of History at the University of Chicago, will tell you of Lincoln's background and his glorious career. Professor Weatherspoon! Ummmmmmmpph! . . . Uuummmmmmmmmphmmm! . . . Good morning, everybody!

I.

No matter how hard he squinted his eyes and craned his neck, he could not see the top of the steps. But somebody was calling and he had to go up. He hollered, *Yeah, I'm coming right up, in just a minute!* And then he started. It was hard work, climbing steps like these. He panted and the calves of his legs ached. He stopped and looked to see if he could tell where the steps ended, but there were just steps and steps and steps. *Shucks, they needn't be in such a helluva hurry,* he thought as he stretched his legs and covered three and four steps at a time. Then, suddenly, the steps seemed funny, like a great big round barrel rolling or a long log spinning in water, and he was on top treading for all he was worth and that voice was still calling. He stopped again, disgusted. *Hell, there just ain't no end to these steps! I'm just wasting time! Ain't moving a peg! And that old sonofabitch up there sounds just like my boss, too!*

Jake stirred and burrowed his head deeper into a pillow. He sighed, swallowed, pulled his knees up, and turned his face from the sun glare.

The steps blazed and shivered in a mist of bright gold, as if about to vanish. Then they grew real and solid. He was still running, thinking: *That guy's still calling. What in hell can he be wanting?* He hollered again, *Keep your shirt on, for Chrissakes! I'm coming!* He was flying up steps now, mounting whole blocks of steps, miles and miles of steps, but even at that the end was not in sight. *What to hell? There's a joke here somewhere! Damn tooting!* He stopped, sighed, wiped sweat from his forehead, and looked to see how many steps he had covered. He was right where he had started! He shook his head, mumbling to himself, *Jeeesus, all that running for nothing . . . Yeah, there's a trick in this.* But that guy, that guy who had a voice like his boss, was still calling.

Jake turned and lay on his stomach. His head rested in the crook of his right elbow. His left arm clung close to his side, dingy palm upcurled. He smacked his lips softly, as though over a dainty and dissolving morsel.

The steps stretched endlessly up. He was taking them five at a time now, not even pausing for breath. A deep sweet gladness suffused his limbs. He would get there soon if he kept this up. All steps ended somewhere. He yelled, *I'm coming! I'm coming!* Then the voice boomed so loud in his ears he stopped and tried to make out what it was saying.

Jake struggled out of sleep and propped himself upon an elbow. A pair of piggish eyes blinked at sunlight. Low growls escaped his half-parted lips and his hands fumbled comically for the runaway sheet. He swallowed several times and his Adam's apple jumped up and down from his chin to his collarbone, like a toy monkey on a string. His eyes smarted, watering. He saw the bed and the dresser and the carpet and the walls melting and shifting and merging into a blur. His loins felt heavy and exhausted. He closed his eyes and his mind groped, thinking, *What was I dreaming?* He remembered being on the very brink of something, on the verge of a deep joy. *Now what was I dreaming?* He tried to think, but a wide gap yawned in his mind. And that guy was still calling.

> . . . Garrison, forerunner of Lincoln, was a man whose soul was aflame with a holy cause. Going against the advice of his friends and the warnings of his enemies, he declared himself outspokenly against slavery and oppression. . . .

Gawddamn! That old radio woke me up! A vague sense of rows and rows of steps came again. *Now what was I dreaming?* It seemed very, very important that he should remember. He screwed up his eyes, but the dream steps were drowned in a vast blackness, like a slow movie fadeout. He had been going somewhere in a great big hurry; he had been thirsting, longing for something. But each time he had got almost to it, each time it was almost his, somebody had called.

> . . . I am in earnest—I will not equivocate—I will not excuse—I will not retreat a single inch—and I will be heard. . . .

Jake's mouth twitched. He flung one black leg from under the sheet and groaned. The air of the room was close. Heat was melting tiny cakes of grease in his nappy hair. He raised his hand and scratched at a thin stream of slickness oozing down the ebony nape of his neck. His face wrinkled, he opened his mouth and bawled:
"Lil!"
"Hunh?"
"Shut that door!"
"Hunh?"
"Shut that Gawddamn door, I said!"
He heard the door slam. *That bitch! How come she leave that door open and wake me up?* He settled down again and the mood of his dream came back. He imagined his loins

10

straining against a warm, nude body. He breathed softly as the muscles of his diaphragm grew taut. A hot, melting ball glowed in his solar plexus. His head drooped and his lips touched the starched pillowcase. He doubled his legs, bringing his knees to the pit of his stomach. He felt the warm body pressing close to him, covering him, heating his blood. *Milkman! Milkman!* He jumped. *Gawddamn!* It was no use; he could not sleep anymore. Through a six-inch opening in the window came the harsh throb of an auto motor. He sat up, his eyes meeting a glare of sunshine pouring slantwise through voile curtains. *Gawd, is it morning already?* He wagged his head and tried to swallow a nasty taste. He made a wry face and tried again. *Arrrrrk! Naw.* He simply could not swallow it. He eased down again, his head striking a sharp edge. He fumbled with his hand and brought before his eyes a small, yellow booklet. UNITY, he read. A MAGAZINE DEVOTED TO CHRISTIAN HEALING. He saw the picture of a haloed, bearded man draped in white folds; the man's hand was resting upon the blond curls of a blue-eyed girl. Beneath the picture ran a caption: EVERY HOUR OF THE DAY AND NIGHT JESUS FLOWS ALL THROUGH ME. *What makes Lil keep all this trash in bed?* He hurled the book across the room, hearing the leaves flutter with a dry sound.

He stood up, dazed somewhat from sleep. He licked his lips and rubbed his eyes with the backs of his hands. His mouth gaped, revealing two rows of gleaming gold. It gaped wide. Wider. Wider still. Then it closed slowly, emitting a hippopotamic grunt, *Yyaaarph!* His eyes watered sympathetically as he stood rigid with his head tilted backward. *Jeeesus, I feel rotten.* He drew a long breath; something itched deep in his nose. Then it came:

"Ker . . . ker . . . kerchoossneeeeze!"

He bent double. When he straightened he wiped his nose and eyes on the sleeves of his red-gold pyjamas, and groaned:

"Aw, hell. . . ."

He was thirsty and his mouth tasted salty. He licked his lips and swallowed again to get rid of that disgusting taste. Adding to his sluggish confusion was a sickening hunger. His stomach felt like a vacuum with a black rat gnawing around inside of it. He got a cigarette from his pack and struck a match. His fingers trembled so the flame flickered out. *My nerves is just all shot,* he thought. When the cigarette was lit he screwed up his eyes and scratched himself, slowly, along the ribs, deep in the groin, around the navel, and between the thighs. He wanted a little more sleep, just a little more. But he knew it was useless. *How come Lil leave that door open? How come she turn that radio on so early?* He flushed hot with anger, but the smell of boiling coffee and

11

sizzling bacon cooled him. He sighed, looking aimlessly around the room, at the curtains, at the sunshine, at the blooming red flowers in the carpet. His attention centered on his scheme rack, a little honeycomblike wooden case before which were piled hundreds and hundreds of tiny white cards. *Lawd, I ain't fooled with that scheme in almost a month now. And I got to go up and pass a test on it in about two weeks.* Merely to think of it made his head feel heavy. He had to learn that scheme, learn where each card went, and when it went where it went, and on what train. *Let's see now. Six o'clock sweat. Chicago and Evans. 15. Number 2. Except on Sundays. That's for Paris, Illinois. Then at nine-thirty comes Chicago and Evans. 9. Number 2. Let's see now. That's except Saturdays. Then comes ten forty-five. Yeah, that's Danville and Cairo. 131. No. 1. That goes by way of. . . .* He frowned, screwing up his eyes and biting his lips. *Where do that Danville and Carbondale go?* He could not remember. And he had nine hundred little white cards like that to commit to memory. Well, he would try to study a little after breakfast. After he had eaten a good meal his mind would be fresh and keen.

As in a dream he ambled to the bathroom, his fat black feet spreading like cobra heads upon the carpet. He turned the cold water faucet in the washbowl and looked around for a glass. *That bitch! How come she can't never do nothing right? You can never find a thing you want when she's around!* Stooping, he cupped his fingers under the stream and gulped huge swallows of water overflowing the brim of his palms. *Yeah, I feel lots better now.* He stood up, fronting the mirror. The reflection showed a face round as a full moon and dark as a starless midnight. In an oily expanse of blackness were set two cunning eyes under which hung flabby pouches. A broad nose squatted fat and soft, its two holes gaping militantly frontward like the barrels of a shotgun. Lips were full, moist, and drooped loosely, trembling when he walked. A soft roll of fat seeped out of his neck, buttressing his chin. Shaggy sideburns frizzled each temple.

He ran his fingers through his hair, scratching an itchy scalp. He brought them away sticky and greasy. Thrusting out his jaw, he touched bristles on his chin. He needed a haircut and a shave. Badly. *Shucks, how come you got to waste a hour getting your hair cut? How come you got to shave every day?* He took down his mug and shaving brush and turned on the hot water. Wisps of vapor warmed his chest and face. *Christ, that feels good!* The smell of coffee and sizzling bacon became stronger. Slowly, he was waking up; even his mind began to work a little.

12

He cocked his head, poising his whitely lathered brush an inch from his chin. He heard Lil talking to somebody in the kitchen. He bent lower, listening. *What in hell can she find to talk about all the time? I certainly would like to know. And bawling her out don't seem to do a bit of good, neither. Yeah, she's going to keep on with her foolishness till I teach her a damn good lesson one of these days. And furthermore, it ain't right for a decent woman to stand talking common that way to strangers. And she knows that!* Jake sat the mug down, hurried to the bathroom door, and listened with his ear to the keyhole. *Still talking! And laughing, too! What to hell? What she think this is, a picnic?* He slammed down the brush and pushed through the door.

He entered the kitchen just as Lil threw back her head, laughing. Her shoulders were shaking. But when she saw Jake she sobered. The milkman hastily picked up his rack.

"Good morning," said the milkman.

Jake did not answer. He came and stood in the middle of the floor, his legs wide apart.

"You up already, Jake?" Lil asked in a strained voice.

Jake shook his head, his mouth twisting into a crooked smile. "Naw, I'm still asleep."

Lil fumbled for a dishtowel and began to polish an already glittering spot on the stove. The milkman groped for the doorknob.

"Well, I reckon I'll be getting along," he said.

"Be sure and bring me an extra pint of cream tomorrow," said Lil.

"O.K.," said the milkman, and was gone.

Jake slouched heavily into a chair and frowned at the floor. Lil went to the icebox and got a carton of eggs. She bit her lip and kept her shoulders stiff, as though expecting a blow.

"Lil?" His voice held a familiar, ominous portent.

She lowered her head an inch and placed a skillet on the stove. As she lit the gas her face was placid, as though she had not heard. Sometimes that forestalled him, pretending like that.

"Lil!" Anger was creeping into his voice.

"I hears you, Jake." She spoke placatingly.

"Act like it then!"

She broke an egg into the skillet. Jake's toes gripped the linoleum as though even they were angry with her.

"Woman, I'm still talking to you!"

She sprinkled salt over the egg.

"What's wrong with you?"

"Nothing."

"Don't you hear me talking?"

13

"Yeah, I hears you, Jake."

"Why in hell don't you act like it?"

She broke a second egg. A part of the white caught on the edge of the skillet and hardened slowly. Jake rose from his chair.

"Is you deaf?"

"Naw, I ain't deaf. I hears you real plain."

"I just wanted to know," he said. "On account of if you was, I can fix you so you can hear real good from now on."

His face was six inches from hers.

"What in hell can you see in a milkman's mug to make you want to keep talking to him all day—that's what I want to know!"

Lil cleared her throat, bent lower over the skillet, and fiddled the eggs with a long-handled fork.

"Now, listen, woman, I'm talking to you!"

"Nothing," she answered. "I don't see nothing."

"How come you keep talking to him?"

Business of turning the first egg over. Jake gripped her shoulder, pulling her from the stove.

"Ain't you going to talk to me?"

"Please, Jake, for Chrissake, let's don't start all that again!"

"Start what? What in hell you mean? Is you crazy! You's the one what's starting! Ain't I told you about that milkman before, a dozen times if one?"

Tenderly, Lil flipped the second egg over with a wide paddle. Jake gripped her arm, digging long nails into her flesh.

"I'm talking to you, bitch!"

"Yes, Jake."

"Ain't I told you about that milkman before?"

"Yes, Jake."

"How come you keep talking to him?"

Lil turned and faced him meekly. Her shoulders slumped as if she were placing all evidence before him for an impartial judgement, as if she were throwing herself upon his mercy, his ultimate sense of fairness.

"What you want me to do, Jake? Act like I'm wild? Can't I say good morning to folks when they say good morning to me? Honest to Gawd, I said no more to that milkman than I do to Mrs. Thomas. . . ."

"I ain't no fool! I heard you talking to that milkman ten minutes on end! I reckon he can't hear good, hunh? I reckon it takes ten minutes to tell him to bring you a bottle of cream, hunh? Woman, don't you try to play me cheap!"

"I ain't playing you cheap."

14

"You turned that radio on so I wouldn't hear what you was telling him!"

"Lawd, Jake. . . ."

"Now just say you didn't!"

She gaped at him.

"I ain't blind! I can see what's going on before my eyes! You can't put a damn thing over on me, and ain't no use you trying. And I reckon that sweet laugh you gave him was part of the order, too, hunh?" He swayed his body forward, his face leering.

Lil sighed.

"I sure wish you wasn't so foolish, Jake."

He shoved her from the stove again.

"Don't you call me a fool!"

"I didn't call you a fool!"

"Watch out how you talk to me!"

"I wish you could look at things sort of straight."

"I can look straight enough to see what you doing!"

Lil turned on him. As she spoke her whole body shook as though she had lost control of her nerves. She seemed impelled by an imperious, inner need.

"Just 'cause you so loose you think everybody's loose! If you was half as fair with me as I is with you, we wouldn't never fuss. But it's just like a person who's cheating to think another one is. . . ." She stopped abruptly, choking. "And you know . . . you know . . . you know I ain't in no condition to dddo wwwhat yyyou thinking. . . . You. . . ." The muscles in her throat grew tight with resentment and she could not go on.

"Aw, cut the sob stuff! It don't work with me! You ain't as sick as you always trying to make out! You can always do everything you want to do but *that*!"

"You ought to be 'shamed!"

"Aw, I'm on to you! You just done made up your mind that you ain't going to be no good to me, that's all. But don't you think you putting that much over on me!" He measured a distance of half an inch on his thumb and forefinger. "I know what you up to! You just one more no good woman, that's all!"

"If I is, you the cause of it! You the cause of it! You the cause of it!" she repeated monotonously.

"Shut up!"

"You the cause. . . ."

"I said shut up!"

The words died in her throat.

"You ain't no good and you ain't never been no good! You been that way every since I married you! And don't think

15

it's just lately I noticed it, neither! Even before you started going to that Gawddamn doctor you was no good!"

Lil clutched convulsively at her apron. Her fork tinkled to the floor. She picked it up and faced him again, her eyes swollen now with tears. She panted her words, her eyes wide.

"Naw, I ain't no good! And I thank my Gawd in Heaven I'll never be no good to you no more! And I hopes to Christ I'll never be! I ain't no good and I thank Gawd now! I'm sick! Yeah, I'm sick! And you the cause of it. So when you think of wanting any of me just remember you the cause of it! You tricked me! You knows you did! You knowed I didn't know what was happening to me when you fooled me into going to that old quack doctor. . . . Now you black and evil enough to try to take it all out on me. . . . Maybe I'll never be well again. . . . I wished I had gone on and had that baby than bbbe aaall mmmessed up this way. . . ."

Her knees sagged. She was crying hard now. Jake watched her closely with eyes that glittered.

"You ain't no good and you ain't never been no good!"

She turned her face to the window to cheat him of the satisfaction of her tears. Eggs were burning and the kitchen was filling with smoke.

"Tend to your cooking, you slut! I reckon you think I ought to be happy standing here watching my money burning up on a skillet!"

"I can't do nothing when yyyou kkkeep on bbobothering me!"

"Shut up and cook!"

She dried her eyes, and, coughing because of the smoke, dumped the charred eggs into a garbage pail, and washed the skillet.

"You can do everything you want to do but tend to your own business!" he told her with deep gravity.

He was quiet because he had won; she was quiet because she had lost. But neither was quit of the other. He knew that she would not take the last word. And she felt that he was not yet satisfied with what he had done. Silently, both searched for words that would wound. Seconds passed. Lil found such words first.

"Jake," she began quietly, "you better make a payment to the doctor. I had to go to see him yestiddy and the bill was almost five hundred dollars. He ain't been paid a thing in almost a month now, and it's getting long past due."

He turned away, waving a scornful palm.

"Tell him I ain't got no money."

"You get paid day after tomorrow."

"That's none of your Gawddamn business!"

16

"Well, you just as well pay him now. He says I got to have a operation, and the bill'll be twice as big."

"Got to have *what*?"

"A operation."

"Operation?"

"I got to be operated on in a month."

"When he tell you that?"

"Yestiddy, when I saw him."

"Operated on for what?"

"He says I got a tumor."

"Tumor?"

"Yeah, a tumor!"

Jake looked at her as though he had never seen her before.

"What in hell you doing going getting a tumor?"

"I done run off too many times fooling with you! That's how come I got it!"

"That's a Gawddamn lie!"

"Well, the doctor says so!"

"That's just your little red wagon, then!"

"He says it'll cost five hundred dollars, and that's just *your* little red wagon!"

"Yeah," Jake said through clenched teeth. "I can just see myself giving that damn quack five hundred dollars for you to get rid of a tumor. What you think I is, the United States' Mint? And you got the nerve to tell me I'm the cause of it! How about all the other niggers you been running around with?"

"There ain't been nobody but you!"

"Tell that quack he can get my money when hell freezes over!"

"If you don't pay 'im he can get your job!"

Jake's eyes went red. She had touched his sore spot—his government job. Her complaint on him at the Post Office would throw him out of work. Twice before she had complained, and one more time would just about put an end to him.

"You mighty damn eager to pay that quack. You ain't no good to me but you's a plenty damn good to him. You been going to that sonofabitch a long time, almost seven years. I can't make out what in hell he's doing to keep treating you all this time. . . ."

"Whatever he's doing's all your fault and you got to pay for it!"

"I done ask you for the last time to shut up!"

He stiffened. His jaws clamped vicelike. He wanted to slap her, slap her a blow that would make her hold her mouth forever. But he could not do that without being egged on more. He had reached that point where deep in him he longed for her to goad him just a little more, just a bit more. He wanted ever so badly to slap her, but he wanted to feel impelled. He trembled. His eyes wandered nervously about the kitchen, seeking for a clue, for a point of departure. Suddenly, he felt the emptiness of his stomach and remembered his hunger.

"Quit your Gawddamn jawing and put something to eat on my table!"

Lil looked at him quietly.

"You ain't washed. You ain't ready to eat yet."

Something tightened in him. All the hate of his marriage welled up. Lil seemed to have gone far beyond the power of his words to cut and wound.

"If you don't like the way I'm running this show, why in hell don't you get out?"

Lil poured cream into a pitcher.

"I'm staying 'cause this is my home, and you going to support me! Don't think you going to get out of it, neither, not long as you working. . . ."

Nails bit into palms. If he could only think of something to say to her that would make her so mad she would get up and leave, something so hot and hard that she would never want to forgive him, never want to see him again—something that would get rid of her once and for always.

"I can't see how come any slut wants to be hanging around a man who don't want her, I just can't see. . . ."

"I knows you can't see, but I'm staying! I knows you don't want me, but you going to support me!"

He rammed his hands into the pockets of his pyjamas, and leaned against the window casing.

"And suppose I don't support you?"

"Then I'll go down to that Post Office and tell 'em!"

"The day you go down to that Post Office and snitch on me again, that's the day you going to be sorry!"

"And the day you stop paying these bills that's the day you going to be sorry!"

He came to her side.

"I done took about enough off of you!"

"You ain't through taking yet!"

"Shut up, you lowbellied slut!"

"If I'm a slut now I was one when you married me!"

"I didn't want you in the first place!"

"You had a funny way of showing it!"

"If you hadn't lied and said you was big, I wouldn't've never married you, neither."

"You went around with your tongue lapping out to get me," said Lil, placing knives and forks upon the table.

18

"Don't cross talk me, woman!"

"You did!"

"Listen, pack your duds and get going! I don't want you!"

"Make me!"

"I don't want you, hear me!"

"And I don't want you, neither! All I want from you is support, and I'm going to get it or get your job!"

He leaned over her, his eyes fastened on her bare neck, his hands hanging limply at his sides.

"You can't talk this way to me!"

"Then don't talk to me!"

A hot sense of elation bubbled in him. He felt the muscles of his back stiffening. Just a few more words from her, just a few more, and, by God, he would slap her into the middle of next Christmas. His right hand itched. His voice dropped to a low growl.

"I'm asking you for the last time to shut up!"

Lil knew she was risking danger, but she could not resist.

"Make me!"

She dodged, but too late. Jake's open palm caught her square on her cheek, sounding like a pistol shot. She spun around from the force of the blow, falling weakly against the wall, screaming.

"Don't you hit me no more! Don't you hit me no more!"

He was at her side, his raised palm open and threatening.

"I said shut up!"

She ducked and let out a sharp scream. He jerked her from the wall. She stumbled into the middle of the floor, barricading her face behind arms and elbows.

"I ask you to shut up!"

As she screamed again, he brushed her arms aside and slapped her a quick onetwo with the front and back of his palm on both sides of her face. She sank to her knees, her bosom too full to utter a sound.

"Ain't you going to shut up!"

He stood over her, his legs wide apart, his hands dug deep into his pockets, looking at her heaving bosom.

"Get up!"

"I'm going to fix you," she sobbed. "So help me Gawd, I'm going to fix you. . . ."

"I said get up!"

He kicked her in her side with his foot.

"This is the last time you going to do this to me!"

"I told you to get up! You act like you want some more!"

He bent over to slap again. Quickly she dragged along the

floor out of his reach, and pulled to her feet, turning her face from him.

"You want some more?"

"Naw, Jake. . . ."

He caught her left wrist in his right hand.

"Tell me what you going to do about it?"

"Jake, please. . . ."

"Tell me what you going to do about it?" he asked again, twisting her arm slowly up her back.

"Turn me loose!"

He gave her arm a six-inch twist. Pain made her suck her breath in sharply. She fell to her knees.

"You breaking my arm!"

"Tell me what you going to do about it?"

"Nothing," she breathed. "Nothing."

He shoved her from him.

"Put something to eat on my table before I give you some more!"

Sniffing and blinded by tears, she fumbled for the handle of the coffee pot.

II.

He lumbered back to the bathroom, massaging his tingling palms and mumbling to himself. He had slapped Lil so hard his fingers felt cold. But deep in him he knew he had not done what he wanted; he had not solved anything. *This bitch is ruining me,* he thought as he stared at the white lather drying on his shaving brush. She was taking every ounce of joy out of his life. She had piled up a big doctor's bill, a bill so big that it seemed he could never pay it. Then she had gone like a fool and burned up his eggs, eggs that cost cold, hard cash. *And on top of that she goes and gets herself a Gawddamn tumor!* He slammed the brush into the bowl and turned on the hot water. Each week his bills were mounting; each week he was falling further behind. He gritted his teeth. *That bitch!*

About him sunshine poured through green curtains, splashed the white bathtub, glinted on the metal faucets and shivered in little ghostly patches on the tile floor. He softened his brush and looked miles deep into the white tiles, thinking: *If Lil goes and has that operation it'll put me almost a thousand dollars in debt to that doctor. And that ain't counting all the other bills I owe, neither. And if I don't pay 'em they'll kick me off my job. . . .* A wave of self-pity swept through him. *What to hell? What in the*

20

world can a man do? I'm just like a slave. . . . He owed so many debts he did not know which debt to pay first. And a thousand dollar doctor bill would just about fix him for good. If he went to a loan bank and borrowed a thousand dollars, how long would it take him to pay it back? *Let's see now,* he thought, moving his lips silently. *If I pay back two and a half on each payday, that'll make five dollars a month. Let's see now. Five dollars a month? Twelve months in a year. Five times twelve is . . . is. . . . Let's see now. Five times two is ten. Write your naught and carry your one. Five times one is five, and one to carry makes six. Yeah, sixty dollars. Sixty dollars a year.* Now how many years would it take him to pay that off? In his imagination he pictured the numeral one and annexed three naughts. He then drew two long white lines and placed the figure sixty to the left. *Now let's see. Six into ten goes how many times? That's right! One! And six from ten leaves four. All right, go on and bring down the naught, making it forty. And six into forty goes. . . . Let's see now.* He screwed up his eyes as he had done long years ago when standing at the blackboard in grammar school. *Six into forty goes. . . . Four times six is twenty-four. And five times six is thirty. And six times six is thirty-six. Yeah, six times. And there's just a little left over. But that don't matter much. The main thing is that it'll take sixteen years. . . . Sixteen years! Good Gawd!* Then there were other bills: the furniture bill and the rent bill and the gas bill and the light bill and the bill at the Boston Store and the insurance bill and the milk bill. His eyes grew misty with tears, tears of hatred for Lil and tears of pity for himself. *My life is just all shot to hell. I wouldn't be in all this mess if it wasn't for her. She ain't no good no way I can figger it!*

He was broke. There was but one way out; he would have to go to somebody, like Jones, maybe, and borrow enough to tide him over till the fifteenth of the month. But even if he borrowed he would not pay the doctor today. *I'll be Gawddamned if I pay that quack today! Naw, naw, not today!* He had already promised Al and Bob and Slim he would stand the treats tonight. He could not get out of that so easily. It was his turn, and what kind of a sport would he be if he held them up? *They'll call me cheap. Aw, to hell with that quack! He'll just have to wait, that's all! Ain't no sense in a man working himself to death just to pay a quack doctor bill. And if Lil gets smart and tries any of them sly tricks of hers. . . .* He swallowed.

He whipped the brush around in the mug, thinking, *And what to hell! She oughtn't be so damned worried, nohow. Ain't she always reading Unity books? Ain't she always talk-*

ing about how she trusts Gawd? Yeah, she ought to ask Gawd to get rid of that tumor for her. His face softened. Out of the soil of his anger an idea bloomed. *The very next time she tells me about that damned tumor I'll tell her to let Unity take care of it. Let them bastards send up a silent prayer! Give her a dose of her own sweet medicine!* He smiled, his wounded vanity soothed.

His temper subsided and he turned to the mirror. *Can't I put off shaving 'til tomorrow? My face don't look so bad, do it?* He touched the stiff bristles, reflectively. *Naw, I can't go round all day with my face looking like this.* He caught more hot water and lathered his brush. The bristles rustled with a dry sound as he mopped his chin. Whitened, he opened the medicine cabinet and searched the shelves. *Where's my razor?* The last time he had used it he had left it in here, right behind the iodine. He pushed back cold cream jars and blue-green bath salts. No razor. *That bitch!*

"Lil!"

"Hunh?"

"Where in Gawd's name you hide my razor?"

"Razor?"

"Yeah, razor! Is your ears stopped up?"

Lil came to the bathroom door with a salt shaker in one hand and a dishtowel in the other. Her eyes avoided him.

"Come on in here, woman, and find my razor! Can't you see I'm *waiting!*"

"Just a minute. . . ."

"Where you put my razor?"

"I seen it somewhere. . . ."

"*Put,* you mean. How come you hide it, anyhow?"

"I didn't hide. . . ."

"Why can't you leave my things where they belong?"

Lil jammed the salt shaker into her apron pocket and went into the bedroom. Jake ambled after, scowling.

"How come you looking in here?"

"I'm trying to remember where I put it. . . ."

"Remember?" he growled. "Remember? Yeah, like you remember burning eggs under your nose."

"Jake, give me a second. . . ."

"Give you hell! Get my razor!"

Absent-mindedly, she banged drawers, pulled up a dresser scarf, and glanced under a pillow. Jake came to her side.

"What you looking under that pillow for?"

"Honest to Jesus, Jake, I'm trying to think. . . ."

He grabbed her arm.

"Who was here yestiddy after I was gone?"

Her shoulders slumped. Jake placed one hand firmly about her throat.

22

"You want me to open your mouth to see if you got a tongue?"

"Naw, Jake."

"What in hell make you want to hide my razor?"

She tried to answer, but he tightened his fingers.

"Can't you talk, you dumb bitch!"

"Jake, nnnobody wwwas hhhere. . . ."

"You lying!"

"I cccross my hhheart and sssswear. . . ."

He pushed her to the wall.

"Find my razor before I choke you into a black spasm!"

Meekly, she searched. Finally, both to her surprise and Jake's, she found the razor under a shallow dish upon the dresser. He snatched it from her.

"Jake, don't you remember you left it in here yestiddy?"

He remembered, but the mere act of remembering made him angrier.

"Did I ask you anything?"

"Naw, but you. . . ."

"Then hold your old big mouth till I speak to you!"

Lifting the razor to the light, he examined it. Unchipped. He squinted his eyes, but he could not even see a tiny hair. If he could only find just one little nick! But not one! He could scarcely keep the irritation out of his voice.

"Get back in the kitchen and keep your hands off of my things, hear me? If you don't I'm going to fix you good one of these mornings!"

He stropped the razor, shaved, nicked himself, cursed, and jabbed the wound with a styptic pencil. He inspected the tiny scratch minutely, wondering if it would disfigure his face in any way. *Yeah, that bitch! She's always making me nervous. I wouldn't've cut myself if it hadn't been for her damn dumbness!*

But when he was in the tub his anger ebbed. The warm water laved his loins. He stretched out, closed his eyes, and let his body soak. He kicked his legs, revelling in the feel of suds. On drifting wisps of vapor his mind winged away. Deep in the tile walls he saw the dim outlines of a soft, brown body. His eyelids drooped. The water lapped at his diaphragm and his flesh swooned in oozy eddies. A sweet lump rose in his stomach and traveled upwards, filling his throat. He lifted the washrag and squeezed it slowly, making the water trickle against his skin. His lips sagged and he sighed. The woman's body hovered nearer, growing in solidity. Uneasily, in spite of himself, he stirred; the delicious feeling petered out. He shook his head and studied the shiny soap bubbles, thinking, *Jeeesus*. He sang:

23

> *"I woke up too soon*
> *The spell was broken*
> *I woke up too soon*
> *Ending a dream*
> *You were so beautiful*
> *So wonderful*
> *And so divine*
> *There was such tenderness in your caress*
> *You were almost mine. . . ."*

As he soaped his armpits and groin:

> *"You took away my soldiers when you took away your love*
> *You said it was a plaything I wasn't worthy of*
> *You packed away my soldiers on a shelf way up above*
> *And I'm just little boy blue. . . ."*

> *You took away my candy when you took away your kiss*
> *I never thought to lose a thing would make me feel like*
> * this*
> *But now I know you took away the thing I'll always miss*
> *And I'm just little boy blue. . . ."*

He dried himself, pulled on his BVD's, socks, and washed his hands in a stream of sunshine. He felt good, but the bathtub mood still lingered.

> *"Got me doing things, things I never thought I'd do-oo-oo*
> *Got me doing things, some are silly, some are new-oo-oo*
> *Got me saying things, things I never said before-o-o*
> *Got me saying things like you're the one I adore-o-o. . . ."*

He next tackled the big job of the morning. His hair had to be combed, combed flat so that not a ripple, not a crinkle, not a crease must show. Going to the mirror, he surveyed the unruly strands with the apprehensive air of a veteran field marshal inspecting the fortifications and wire-entanglements of an alien army. He wore his hair in the style of Negro bangs. His nappy forelocks reared fanwise in a wooly black flare which had to be bullied into a billiard ball smoothness.

Years of dealing with this foe had taught him many devices of strategy. The first barrage was with water, and plenty of it. Going to the washbowl, he dampened his hair till rivulets streamed down his neck. Then, seizing his comb like a Colt .45, he tried to force an opening through enemy lines. The battle waxed furious. The comb suffered heavy losses, and fell back slowly. One by one teeth snapped until they littered bathmat and washbowl. Mangled and broken things they lay there, brave soldiers fallen in action, many of them clutched in the death grip of enemy hairs. After three minutes of attack the strands abandoned their trenches and retreated disorderly.

Jake now brought forth the most powerful weapon at his command. This deadly contraption was a pink jar of hair pomade labeled, LAY 'EM LOW. Its chief ingredient was a stout beeswax, a substance as fatal to insurgent kinks as was mustard gas in Flanders. He rammed his forefinger deep into the jar and pulled forth on a nail a dab of yellow stickiness the size of a walnut. He smeared it vigorously between his palms, and delivered a sudden broadside. Not a man fell. Only with the impact of a second assault did a few waver or weaken. Tightening his lips and spreading his fingers, he launched drive upon drive till the brave fellows broke at the knees. Then he pinned them tight, pummelled them into a foul and gluey morass.

He was breathing hard. He resorted to the comb again. A hot skirmish on the left and right flanks had each warweary strand clinging to his scalp like troops in shell holes under bombardment. The enemy was conquered! Jake peered into the mirror. His head was a solid mass of black slickness. He smiled, thinking with satisfaction *If a fly'd light on that he'd slip up and break his neck. . . .*

He went into the bedroom and looked through the pockets of his trousers for a stocking cap. This ingenious implement of exploitation, this standing army which a conquering nation leaves to guard a conquered one, is made from the top of a woman's stocking. It is elastic, about four inches long, tied securely at the top, and when stretched tightly over the cranium resembles the gleaming skin of a huge onion. He was in a hurry, for, failing to get his hair under this peace treaty immediately, it would soon flounce back into a thousand triumphant kinks. He searched in vain. After a few minutes he stood in the middle of the room, empty-handed, angry-eyed.

"Lil!"

No answer.

"Liiiil!"

No answer.

"Woman, you hear me calling!"

Still no answer. His voice swelled throughout the flat like the roar of a lion.

"Liiiiiiiiiiiiiiiil!"

"Just a minute, Jake."

She came leisurely to the door.

"Where was you?"

25

"On the back porch."

"You don't belong there."

"I. . . ."

"How come you didn't answer when I called?"

"I didn't hear you. . . ."

"Running your old fat mouth like always, hunh?"

She hung her head.

"Who was you talking to this time?"

"Mrs. Thomas."

"What in hell can you find to talk about all the time?"

She swallowed and sighed.

"Tell me what you want, Jake. I'm cooking breakfast."

"Well, just you wait awhile now. If you got time enough to gab with that Thomas bitch then you got time enough to wait till I tell you what I want." He continued to smooth his hair down with the palms of his hands.

Lil closed her eyes and leaned weakly against the bedpost.

"Where's my stocking cap?"

"Stocking cap?"

"Yeah, stocking cap! Stocking cap! Stocking cap! Can't you never understand nothing?"

"I don't know, Jake. I ain't had it. I don't need no cap like that nohow." Complacently she patted her own smooth and kinkless hair.

"What you trying to signify?"

He advanced a step.

"I ain't trying to signify nothing," she said quickly.

"Well don't, if you knows what's good for you! I done told you I wants a stocking cap!"

"But I ain't got nothing but my new stockings. You done ruined all my stockings already, tearing 'em up for caps. And how you lose so many caps, anyhow?"

"What's that got to do with it? I said I wants a cap!"

"But I ain't got none, Jake!"

"Get one, then!"

"I told you I ain't got nothing but my new stockings!"

"Ain't you going to get me a cap?"

"I ain't. . . ."

"I'll get one!"

He brushed her aside and headed for her dresser.

"Jake, please! Not my new stockings!"

"GET ME A STOCKING CAP!"

She scurried for the clothes closet.

He stood waiting, thinking: She better not fool with me no more today. . . .

She returned with an old hose.

"Here, Jake. You better take good care of this, 'cause if you lose it I ain't got no more."

"Thought you said you didn't have none?"

She averted her eyes and left the room. Tugging, he pulled the cap down over his hair. An hour of pressure would dry the water and grease. His hair would remain in place all day. Going to the mirror, he struck a pose and smiled. Again he sang:

> *"I think of you with every breath I take*
> *And every breath becomes a sigh*
> *Not a sigh of despair*
> *But a sigh that I care for you. . . ."*

III.

Jake stood before the ten suits hanging in his closet and tried to make up his mind. His fingers strayed from one to the other, feeling the texture of the goods. He did not want to wear the black, nor the blue, nor the brown. They were all right, but he just did not want to wear them. He was not in the mood. He shook his head at a grey tweed. It was much too light in color and weight for winter wear. And so was the tan. He passed over three more because they were double-breasted. *Shucks, everybody's wearing double-breasted suits these days.* His choice finally narrowed down to a light green one-button sack and a winereddish ensemble with pleated trousers. He liked the winereddish one because it was so roomy and made him look fifteen or twenty pounds heavier, like a big time football player. *But shucks, I done wore that old suit so much lately.* He fingered the green; he pictured himself swinging along the street in the sunshine. He imagined eyes following him. *Yeah, I'll wear that green.* After he had slid into the trousers, he stood looking down at the keen creases, smiling with critical approval.

"Sharp as a tack," he said.

And because he was wearing the green suit, he decided on low-cut, brown suede shoes with high Cuban heels and toes that tapered to a point. He tied the shoestrings in a neat, tight bow. Spotlessly white spats capped the bargain. Next, he put on a soft-collared lavender shirt which contrasted pleasingly with his broad, red, elastic suspenders. Then he tried a black tie, a green tie, a brown tie, and a red tie. In the end he selected a wide yellow one studded with tiny blue halfmoons. He added a delicate finishing touch by inserting a huge imitation ruby that burned like a smear of fresh blood. Squaring his shoulders, he buttoned coat and vest and adjusted with sensitive fingers the purple embroi-

dered orange handkerchief that peeped out of his breast
pocket. He sprayed each of his coat lapels with violet-scented
perfume, then pivoted on his heels in the middle of the rug
and brought himself to a sudden halt in front of the dresser
mirror.

"Like a Maltese kitten," he said.

*Well, I reckon I'll go in and eat some now, eat a nice,
big, hot breakfast. Then I'll study my scheme some. Yeah, I
got to study that scheme. I can't keep on putting it off and
putting it off all the time. Then I'll walk out awhile. Hunt up
some of the old gang, maybe....*

Breakfast was laid on the kitchen table. He sat down opposite Lil, who was reading a copy of *Unity*, with her face
cupped mournfully in her hands. Jake stared at her, and
then at the turnedback page that faced him. Across the top
of it he saw a wide spread of yellow, Egyptian wings, under
which ran a slogan: A PAGE OF SUNSHINE FOR EVERY DAY. Her
interest in the book irked him. *Every time she pokes her
head into them damn books I can't hardly talk to her.* He
groped for something to say, something that would rouse
her out of her smug complacency. *By Gawd, she sets there
just like I didn't slap her a few seconds ago!* He picked up
the sugar bowl.

"Well?"

Lil lifted her eyes momentarily.

"Hunh?"

"Ain't you eating?"

"Naw."

"What's griping you?"

"Nothing."

"How come you ain't eating?"

"I just ain't hungry."

"Well, I *is*! And you ain't hurting me a damn bit if you
don't *never* eat!"

He sweetened his coffee and sucked a long sip.

"Where my paper?"

Lil fetched the morning's paper from the porch. Rearing
back in the chair, he opened it and read the headline aloud.

ROOSEVELT STRIKES AT MONEY CHANGERS
WILL DRIVE THEM FROM THE TEMPLE, HE SAYS

"Hunh," Jake grunted as he laid the paper aside and took
up a slice of toast. "That's what *he* says! And what he says
is just so much hot air. Nobody'll ever tell these rich American men what to do. Naw siree! Not so long as Gawd's sun
shines. Cold, hard cash runs this country, always did and
always will. You can put that in your hat and bet your bot-

tom dollar on it. And what to hell! Who is these old Democrats, anyhow? I'll tell you what they is! They's crazy troublemakers! They ain't got no money. And what in hell can a man do without money? Tell me that! Nothing! And empty words don't mean a damn thing, neither. Say, who's going to tell old man Morgan and old man Rockefeller and old man Ford what to do? Who? WHO?" Jake stabbed the air with his fork. "Why them men owns and runs the country! And furthermore, these old Democrats is always starting wars. Old Wilson started one, and now they want to put another Democrat in office to start another one. Everybody knows these old Democrats is hotheaded, so why put 'em in office? People's crazy! Crazy with the heat! They don't know white from black! Shucks, old Hoover was doing all right, only nobody couldn't see it, that's all. . . . I'm going to stick with the Republicans. Old Abe Lincoln is the ship and all else is the sea. . . ." Now, who said that? . . .

He frowned, screwing up his eyes. He crammed a piece of toast in his mouth, chewed, and flushed it down with a gulp of coffee. Lil went to the sink and took a tall, dark bottle from a shelf. Jake watched her pour a tablespoon level full.

"What's that you drinking?"

"Medicine," she answered.

"What kind is it?"

"Mrs. Lydia E. Pinkham's Vegetable Compound."

"What you taking it for?"

"My nerves."

"Aw, that stuff ain't doing you no good. You just throwing my money away. . . ."

"I'm sick, Jake."

"You always sick."

She swallowed the medicine.

"I got to take something," she sighed.

Jake jerked his lips, took a mouthful of egg and bacon, and turned to the paper again. *I'm going to stop her from throwing my money away one of these days.* . . .

GERMANY DEMANDS ARMS EQUALITY
VOWS TO BOLT LEAGUE IF DENIED

"See! There she goes! What did I tell you? They's loose again! I always did say they should've wiped them monkeys off the map while they was at it. Them sonsofbitches is sure one slick and trickery lot—I'm here to tell you. I remembers way back during the War when old Reverend Harmond —he's dead now, poor fellow—said that them guys was closer to savages than anybody. And, by Gawd, he sure knowed what he was talking about, too! Yeah, you better watch them German Devils; they's a ornery and lousy lot as sure as you born. You know one thing? They say them German guys got some kind of a poison gas over there that's so strong and powerful that all they got to do is just skeet some of it in the air and when you smell it you'll curl up and die like a chinch! Just think of that! You know, they say them German soljers took them little Beljum babies— little, innocent, newborn babies, mind you, now—raped 'em and stuck 'em with bayonets to telegram posts. How can people do things like that? And shucks, if they happen to come across a French woman, no matter how old she was, that was just too bad. Every soljer in the German army would pile her, and when they got through there wasn't nothing left. Just think now: one soljer after another getting on one poor little woman, and she just laying there and can't do nothing. And ain't no policemen around to bother you. . . ." Jake paused, wagged his head, and gazed deep into the checkered tablecloth. "A soljer gets a chance to do a lot of things. . . ."

He poised a piece of egg on the tip of his fork and squinted at another headline.

G-MEN SPREAD NET FOR GANGSTERS

"Now what's wrong with them Government? What they want to bother them poor guys for? They ain't doing nothing but robbing a few banks. Aw, I know what's wrong with 'em. They's just jealous because they's not splitting their dough with them, that's all. They don't want them gangsters to make so much money. Why, them gangsters is sports, *real* sports. . . . The papers say they ain't never snitched on none of their pals. I was reading just the other day where one of them guys was laying in the hospital dying and the cops was trying to get him to tell who shot 'im and he wouldn't talk, wouldn't say a word. He just looked up at 'em and smiled! By Gawd, it takes guts to die like that. And all the time they's alive they walk around knowing that at any time somebody might shoot 'em down. Jeeesus, it takes nerve to be a gangster! But they have a plenty of fun. Always got a flock of gals hanging on their arms. Dress swell in sporty clothes. Drive them long, sleek automobiles. And got money to throw away. . . . They don't live long, but I bet they sure have a hell of a sweet time while they do live. Better time than a lot of us who work hard every day for a measly living."

He broke a piece of toast and spread it with strawberry jam. As he chewed he watched Lil's eyes following the printed lines of her *Unity*. *That woman's going to read herself blind!* Again he searched for something to say that would rouse her to a sharp sense of his presence.

"I think anybody that don't like gangsters is crazy!" he said loudly.

"Hunh?"

"The government is out after gangsters," said Jake, tapping the paper with his knife.

"Gangsters?"

"Yeah, gangsters, deaf woman!"

Lil stared. Jake laid down his knife, cocked his head, and looked at her with infinite compassion.

"Woman, what makes you so dumb? Don't you never try using your brains sometimes? Don't you never think of nothing that's serious?"

"I don't know, Jake."

"How come you don't know?"

"I wasn't listening to you reading."

"You could learn something if you didn't keep that empty head of yours stuck into them Gawddamn *Unity* books all the time."

Lil's eyes widened.

"Jake, this is Gawd's word!"

"Gawd's hooey! It's a gyp game, that's all!"

"You blaspheming Gawd!"

"So what?"

"Don't you know that Gawd can slap you dead right where you is?"

"Aw, woman, don't be dumb!" he said, glaring as though she had threatened him. "This is the last time you're going to read that stuff in my house, get me? Don't send no more of my money off for that damn trash, you hear?"

Lil swallowed. Jake turned disdainfully to the paper.

HITLER CALLS ON WORLD TO SMASH JEWS

"Now, that's something for everybody to think about. It shows that people's waking up. That's what's wrong with this country, too many Jews, Dagos, Hunkies, and Mexicans. We colored people would be much better off if they had kept them rascals out. Naw, the American white man went to sleep; he didn't have sense enough to let us black people have a break. He had to let them Jews and all in. Now they got the country sewed up; every store you see is run by a Jew, and the foreigners. And they don't think about nobody but themselves. They ought to send 'em all back where they came from. That's what I say."

Jake paused and drained his cup.

"You want some more coffee?"

"Yeah, fill it up."
He stirred his cup and read again.

EINSTEIN SAYS SPACE BENDS

"Humph! Now this is what I call crazy! Yes, siree, just plumb crazy! This guy takes the prize. What in hell do he know about space bending? How in hell can he see space bending when he can't even *see* space? I'm asking you? You know one thing, these old newspapers sure tries hard to fool folks. See, now, a dumb guy would fall for all this kind of stuff. See how folks get their minds made up for 'em? You got to watch sharp and do your own thinking in this old world if you don't want to be fooled. Now, if you ask me, this guy Einstein's just fooling everybody, just saying things to get his name in the papers. Shucks, I could do that. And suppose space do bend, what to hell then? . . . I bet my soul he's a Jew."
Jake turned the page.

COMMUNISTS RIOT IN STREETS OF NEW YORK

"Gawddamn! Wonder how come the police let them guys go on like that? Now them guys, them Commoonists and Bolshehicks, is the craziest guys going! They don't know what they want. They done come 'way over here and wants to tell us how to run *our* country when their *own* country ain't run right. Can you beat that for the nerve of a brass monkey? I'm asking you? Why don't they stay in their own country if they don't like the good old USA? That's what I want to know! And they go around fooling folks, telling 'em they going to divide up everything. And some folks ain't got no better sense than to believe it, neither. Just weak-minded, that's all! Now look here, if I got two suits and another guy ain't got none, they want to take one of mine and let *him* have it! A fool can see that that's wrong! And how are they going to do all this? With bombs and dynamite! What can be wrong with some folks' brains? I wonder! And over in Roosia where they in power, folks is starving to death. And now they want to get us in the same fix. What's wrong with folks when they act like that? If they get in power and tell you to do something and you don't do it, then they lines you up against a wall and shoots you down! That's no lie, I was reading it just the other day in the *Trib-une*. . . ."
"But, Jake!"
"Hunh?"
"Folks is starving over here, too."

"Aw, you talk like a fool!"

"The papers said so."

"Nobody but lazy folks can starve in this country!"

"But they can't get no work."

"They don't want no work!"

"And they burned a colored man alive the other day."

"Who?"

"The white people in this country."

"Shut up! You don't know what you talking about!"

"Well, they *did*!"

"How you know?"

"It was in the papers."

"Aw, that was down South, anyhow."

"But the South's a part of this country."

Jake stopped chewing and glared at her.

"Woman, is you a *Red*?"

Lil blinked. Jake turned back to the paper.

HOODLUMS ABDUCT MILLIONAIRE'S SON

"Well, what you know about that? You see, it just goes to show that rich folks has their troubles just the same as us. After all, it ain't no difference. I'm telling you, Old Man Trouble don't mind nobody. You'd think them folks with all their millions and millions of dollars would be safe and sound from everything. But they ain't, not by a long shot. When you get right down at the bottom of things and start thinking real hard about 'em you begin to see that that's the funny thing about life. When you boil it all low you'll see that everybody gets a equal break in the end. . . ." He looked out of the window, dreamily. "Well, I guess all of us got to get a certain amount of worry in this old world, no matter what. Look like things just works that way, some-how or other. The good Lawd's done got it all figgered out in His own good fashion. It's got to be that way so there can be some justice in this world, I reckon. . . ." His voice trailed off uncertainly.

He drained his cup of coffee, lit a cigarette, leaned his elbows on the table, and sighed. The coffee warmed his blood; he could feel his heart pumping pleasantly. Each time he inhaled the huge breaths of smoke it seemed as though he were going to fall asleep. His head lolled; a lazy thought crawled slowly through his brain. *Lawd, how good it feels after you done eat a good meal.* His eyelids drooped. *Wouldn't it be good now if I could go back to bed and sleep some? Yeah, but that would start Lil's old big mouth again. And I don't want to hear her no more today.* Not that he cared two straws about what Lil would say, but he just did

33

not feel like arguing on a full stomach. It would be much better to go out somewhere, get some fresh air, and loaf around till worktime. Maybe he would walk over to the pool-hall and hear what the old gang was saying. Or maybe he would drop over to Bob's place and play a game or two of bridge. *And I got to get a haircut.* No, he must not forget to get his haircut; he could not be around the sweet girls tonight with hair bristling like cockle burrs on his neck. *Yeah, I'll walk out awhile.* He sighed, his legs feeling deliciously heavy.

"Jake," Lil called humbly from across the table.

He held still, pretending he had not heard. *That bitch is going to ask me for something.* He knew it; he could feel it in his bones.

"Jake," she called again, this time a little louder.

"Hunh?"

"What you want me to fix for dinner?"

"Nothing."

"I got to fix something. So tell me what you want."

"I said *nothing.*"

"Ain't you going to be home for dinner?"

"Naw."

"But I ain't got no money, Jake."

"I told you I wasn't going to be home for dinner."

"I got to have some money. I got to eat, even if you ain't here."

"I ain't got no money!"

"But everything's out! I got to get something."

"What in hell do you do with so much money?"

"I spends it right here in the house for something to eat."

"I give you *two* dollars the other day."

"But that's all gone!"

"Aw, you just throw money away."

"I made two dollars last for three days!"

"Go to the store and ask the man to let you have something on credit."

"The bill up there's so *big.*"

"Ask 'im anyhow!"

"He told me to ask you when you going to pay 'im."

"Tell 'im I'll pay 'im soon."

"We owe so much I'm 'shamed to go there."

"Woman, if you 'shamed to go and ask a man for something to eat, you just stay hungry, see?"

"Jake, please, leave me some money."

"Go to another store and get some groceries."

"I can't!"

"How come? You lame?"

"We owe 'em all bills. They won't let me have nothing."

34

"Listen, for the last time, I ain't got no money! NOW QUIT TALKING TO ME!"

Jake waddled into the living room and slouched across a soft chair; his legs dangled over the sides and his head nestled in the hollow of a pillow. *Gawd, I feel lazy. . . . And that ain't no lie. . . . A good cup of coffee sure makes you feel good.* It made his body languid and made his mind work rapidly. *Jeeesus, if I could only feel this way all the time. . . .*

Dreamily, he looked out the window. The day was dazzlingly bright. That portion of the sky he could see was marvelously blue. Tons of golden sunshine splashed the streets and houses. How queer the drab bricks looked when lit by the light of the sun! The upstretching branches of the trees seemed to be pleading for spring rain. How oddly beautiful it was to be February! A lost spring day set like a jewel amongst the dreary winter ones! *Yeah, it's almost warm enough to go without a winter coat.*

He yawned and scratched his thigh, thinking: *I ought to go in and study my scheme some now. Right now would be a good time to put in some hard work.* But he did not move. His body relaxed; he could feel his toes tingling pleasantly. He gazed drowsily at the keen creases in his trousers, thinking *I don't feel like studying now. Maybe I'll wait till morning. That'll be better. . . .*

A sweet looseness seeped into Jake's bones. He closed his eyes and his blood sogged slowly through his veins like warm milk. He could feel a faint tinge of the sun's warmth even through the windowpane. He pushed his fingers down into his trousers, between his belt and the flat of his stomach. His lips became moist and sagged. His groin felt hot; an uneasy feeling, elusive and light as a feather, played over the surface of his stomach. The muscles of his thighs stretched taut and his mind became hazy. Out of a mist loomed the face of a woman, of *the* woman. The face was brown, winsome, and delicately oval-shaped. Eyelids drooped with languorous passion. Wet lips hovered closer and closer. He could almost see the velvety sheen of her skin. His head swam; his skin glowed as though it were near a soft flame. He doubled his legs as a fugitive feeling of delight burned in his diaphragm. He stirred restlessly, and his shoulders twitched as though he were a child nestling deeper into a mother's bosom. A tiny trickle of saliva drooled out of the corner of his mouth; a look of suspense came into his face . . . .

"Jaaake!"

He jerked, frowned, and wiped his mouth with the back of his hand.

"Hell," he breathed.

35

He closed his eyes and curled himself again, seeking to recapture the lost mood.

"Jaaaaaaake!"

His face contorted savagely.

"What in *hell* you want?"

"You looked in the mailbox yet?"

"Hell, naw! And quit bothering me!"

Again he lowered his head, trying to resuscitate the mood. He was very still, very quiet, but, alas, the mood would not come. *Gawddamit to hell! A man just can't get no rest or peace around Lil.*

He screwed up his eyes, stretched his arms above his head, and yawned.

"Aaaaaaaaahhheellll," he whispered in a breath that seemed to escape involuntarily.

He put on a light grey top coat with huge buttons of liquid pearl and a black hat with a tiny red feather peeping timidly in the back. Grabbing his mahogany-handled cane, he went slowly down the steps, his mind lost in a warm fog.

IV.

In the vestibule he twirled the dial on the mailbox. A bundle of multicolored circulars and advertising throwaways spilled into his hands. He went to the light at the glass door and read the first.

BELIEVE IT OR NOT
a mountain of golden dollars waits for you
$$$$$$ A SURE HIT $$$$$$ A BULL'S EYE BARGAIN $$$$$$ ACT NOW $$$$$$
RISK NOTHING——PAY AFTER YOU WIN

NOTICE—To all number players who are keeping house or can furnish references: Come to see me at once! Bring the year, month, day, and hour of your birth! And I will give you a running gig that will fall immediately. YOU PAY ONLY AFTER YOU WIN! Be sure and bring your last three drawings, and if you have difficulty hitting spiritual gigs I will give you *free* advice as to what to do.

YOU CAN'T LOSE
THE MYSTERIOUS THREESTAR MEDIUM
4545 Vincennes Avenue
Chicago

"Huuuumm. . . . There might be something to this. I'll show it to Lil when I get back; she's always having dreams. But, shucks, she don't keep after nothing what she starts, and you got to keep after these old numbers if you want to win something." He read another:

ASTONISHING$$$$$$ASTOUNDING$$$$$$
UNBELIEVABLE$$$$$$BUT TRUE
LADIES AND GENTLEMEN: LEND ME YOUR EARS!!
I MAKE NUMBERS COME OUT IN ASHES—I MAKE THE
UNSEEN WORLD VISIBLE!

The Second Coming Incense is the most mysterious incense the world has ever known! See for yourself! After the piece has burned you will find numbers in the ashes!

THEY COME STRAIGHT FROM THE SPIRIT WORLD!
Send 50¢ in stamps for a full size trial box,
or $1.00 for a full supply.
YOU CAN'T LOSE!
THE EASTERN CELESTIAL MAGIC COMPANY
3667 South State Street, Chicago

"I ain't never heard of nothing like this before; maybe there's something in it if it comes straight from the spirit world."

Still another:

*VIM AND VIGOR AND VITALITY
FOR ALL MEN AND WOMEN*

Does your back ache? Does your head ache? Are your nerves on edge? Do you feel tired and exhausted all the time? Do you have to get out of bed at night? IF SO, THERE'S HELP FOR YOU AT LAST!

Weak manhood causes a decided change in affections. And this, being not understood, causes mistrust and unhappy homes. LISTEN: YOU SHOULD NOT BE OLD AT SIXTY! If you are suffering from weak manhood or weak womanhood you should take DOCTOR WILLIAM LOUIS SPEEDY'S POWERFUL IMPOTENCY CASTIGATOR FOR MALES AND FEMALES TODAY! It will make a new person or we will give you your money back under our *Golden Seal Moneyback Guarantee*! Just take one bottle and then watch the change that will come over your mate! A full size bottle for only $2.50. Six full size bottles for $12.00.

Send today and avoid worry.
THE DEMOCRATIC PATENT MEDICINE STORE
500 Clay Street
Parson, Pa.

37

(Read the Testimonial below)

Dear Sir:

I began suffering from weak manhood when I was twenty years old. I worried for years. I spent hundreds of dollars on doctors and glandular treatments, but I got no satisfactory results. I gave up; then I heard of DOCTOR WILLIAM LOUIS SPEEDY'S POWERFUL IMPOTENCY CASTIGATOR FOR MALES AND FEMALES. I decided to try it. When I had taken two bottles I underwent a wonderful change, and after taking six bottles I have had no more trouble. It would be hard to find a more popular man than I. I am now sixty years old. You may print this letter if you wish.

Yours humbly,
(Signed) Gabriel Collins
Pastor of the Sunrise Baptist Church

"Shucks, I don't need nothing like this, yet," smiled Jake. And still another:

READ THIS TESTIMONIAL

TO WHOM IT MAY CONCERN:

A year ago, before my twelfth baby was born, I was terribly sick. My feet and legs were swollen to twice their normal size. I had weak, nervous fits and hot flashes. I was so rundown that I once flowed for two months. I was, oh, so irregular and almost died each time with cramps. I had dizzy spells and blind spells. I was despondent and had given up all hope. But every cloud has a silver lining and the darkest hour is just before dawn. And so one morning I found—like a Holy Message from the Great God on High—your card in my mailbox recommending VIRGIN MARY'S NEVERFAIL HERB AND ROOT TONIC FOR NERVOUS AND RUNDOWN WOMEN. I told my husband and doctor about it, and they laughed at me. But since everything else had failed I decided to try it. I was flat on my back when I began taking it. On the second bottle I felt stronger, and was able to set up. Then the great thing happened. My twelfth bottle put me on my feet. I would solemnly swear to these experiences before the UNITED STATES SUPREME COURT. I still use VIRGIN MARY'S NEVERFAIL HERB AND ROOT TONIC FOR NERVOUS AND RUNDOWN WOMEN, and now weigh 203 pounds and still gaining, bless the Lord! You may use this letter if you think it will help others to be saved.

I am yours to sing your praises,
(Signed) Mrs. Cora Saunders
Atlanta, Ga.

ALL WOMEN ORDER YOUR BOTTLE WITHOUT DELAY
TODAY! ONLY $2.00
VIRGIN MARY'S NEVERFAIL HERB AND ROOT TONIC
FOR NERVOUS AND RUNDOWN WOMEN, INC.
534 Fountain Street,
Coldwater, Miss.

"I'm sure going to show this to Lil. This thing might save me some money," Jake mumbled with a quiet sense of elation.

He read the last one:

HE STOPPED HIS WHISKEY DRINKING
by
James' Only Wife

I

I'm the happiest little woman
  In all this little town;
And my merry laugh and singing
  Takes the place of sigh and frown,
For JAMES HAS QUIT HIS DRINKING
  And is like himself once more,
And the world is just a paradise
  With such happiness in store!

II

One day I read some verses—
  Molly's Miracle, the name,
And I said, "That's James exactly,
  And I'll send and get the same."
So I sent for SUREFIRE TREATMENT
  (As sly as sly could be)
And I put it in James' supper
  And I put it in his tea.

III

And it didn't taste a little bit:
  Had no odor, so, you see—
It was the smoothest kind of sailing
  For little Doctor Me.
And I watched and prayed and waited,
  (And cried some, too, I guess)

39

And I didn't have the greatest faith,
I'm ashamed now to confess.

IV

And James never thought a minute
He was being cured of drink,
And soon he's well as any one.
It makes me cry to think!
Just makes me cry for gladness,
I'm so proud to be his wife—
Since he is cured of drinking,
And leads a nice, new life.

V

"Since James he quit adrinking!"
I can't say it times enough!
And hates and loathes a liquor
As he would a poison stuff.
And when I say my prayers at night
As thankful as can be—
I pray for James the most of all—
Then for SUREFIRE TREATMENT!

HOME TREATMENT FOR ALL DRUNKARDS

Odorless and tasteless when used as directed. Any lady can give it secretly at home in tea, coffee, or food.

COSTS YOU NOTHING TO MAKE A TRIAL

If you have a husband, wife, brother, sister, sweetheart, father, mother, or friend who is a victim of liquor, send your name and address on the coupon below. It has helped thousands and should be just the very thing you want. You may be thankful as long as you live that you did it.

THE SUREFIRE TREATMENT COMPANY, INC.
654 Elm Street,
Jackson, Miss.

Very thoughtfully he tore this into tiny pieces and let it filter through his fingers to the tile floor. His lips puckered. *Lil's just crazy enough to want to try this on me if she found it. And there ain't no mail at all. That's right. . . . This is a holiday.* He sorted out the circulars which appealed to him and put them into his pocket. He swung through the door and strolled along the street, drawing from a cigarette. Autos hummed by on rubber tires and their honk-

40

honk seemed real music to him. The air was warm and felt good to his skin. He threw his cigarette away, whistled the refrain from a popular blues song, and jingled the silver coins in his pocket. His mind was as calm as a looking glass. A plump, brown-skinned girl passed; unconsciously he pulled his hat to a rakish angle and jingled his silver louder. He looked up at the wide sweep of blue sky and felt how good it was merely to be alive. As he passed a newsstand his eyes caught for a fleeting moment a black and white picture of a nude, half-charred body of a Negro swinging from the end of a rope. At the top of the picture ran a caption:

DEATH TO LYNCHERS

Jake grunted and whistled louder. He turned a corner and came upon a black boy and a black girl playing upon a pair of tall, wooden steps leading up to an old three-story house.

"I'll beat you up!" one yelled.

"I bet you can't!" the other answered.

Jake watched them scamper up to the top landing. The steps reminded him of something, but he could not tell what it was. He frowned, thinking, *Doggone it, seems like I done forgot something.* He stopped in the middle of the sidewalk and watched the children again. What he was trying to remember hovered on the tip of his tongue; it seemed that in a moment he would speak it. But he could not. He strolled on and lit another cigarette. When he reached the end of the block, when he was no longer trying to remember, it came to him, surged up: the steps, his running, the voice, his whole dream. . . . *Yeah, I want to play my dream. I knowed I was forgetting something. I believe I'll go to the Black Gold Policy Wheel. . . .* He hurried down the block, turned a corner, and knocked softly at a narrow door.

"Who's that?"

"Jake!"

"O.K."

The door swung in.

"What you know, Skinner?"

"Don't know. What you know?"

"Don't know. How's the numbers?"

"Oh, some folks catching and some folks ain't."

The room was crowded, smoky, and there was a low-pitched drone of conversation broken at intervals by shouts. A life-sized pastel of a dark, black-bearded man hung on a rear wall, captioned:

He got a handful of varicolored policy slips from a small table and examined them. They were named *Black Gold, Red Devil, East & West, Interstate, Lucky Strike, Harlem, Bronx, Tia Juana, Old State, Chicago,* and so on. Jake's lips moved silently, recounting what numbers had pulled recently in all the wheels. *Sickrow. . . . Gee, if I knowed about old Lil's operation I could've caught something. Murderrow. . . . Razorrow. . . . Bloodrow. . . . Moneyrow. . . . Looks like these old numbers is falling for somebody. I'm going to see if they'll fall for me.*

He had been playing policy off and on for five years, but had never broken even. He was still behind. How much? He did not know. He played such small sums that he never missed them greatly, and did not bother to keep an account. But he was on the losing side. One time he had caught as high as twenty dollars, and he had played back forty dollars trying to catch twenty more. He would play consistently for about a week and lose consistently, then he would swear off and call the whole thing a fool's game. But a vivid dream would be the signal for his answering again the call of the numbers.

Policy is an elaborate kind of lottery. It is played with 78 numbers, running from 1 to 78, 24 of which are chosen at each drawing to be printed on varicolored slips of paper. Some wheels have one drawing per day, some two, and some as high as three. The 24 numbers on each policy slip are divided into groups of 12 each, and each group of 12 in turn comprises the "leg" of a "book". The player's ability to dream, guess, figure, or otherwise arrive at what three numbers will "fall" in the "leg" of a "book" means that he will win a "gig". A "gig" pays 100 to 1, that is, a dollar for a cent. And who would not take a chance like that?

Of course, Jake had heard that these numbers were capable of being arranged and rearranged to upwards of 70,000 different combinations, and he knew he would never be able to guess or figure out an average rate of recurrence. And he was much too shrewd to trust such a small thing as numbers to fortune tellers, spiritualists, and the like; these people were consulted only in case of a deep, life-and-death crisis. He reasoned correctly that if they could tell him what numbers would "fall", they would play the numbers themselves and get rich. He had a much better and surer scheme; he arrived, or tried to arrive, at the right "gig" through the medium of the dream. He had implicit faith in his dreams; did they not come from some source which no man knew? And for the "key" to his dreams he consulted *King Solomon's*

Wheel of Life and Death Dream Book. There was only one hitch to this: a dream sometimes had so many possible interpretations, it referred to so many different combinations of numbers, that it was impossible to "cover" the dream. Hence, even the dream lost sometimes. But when a dream was especially vivid, like the one he had had last night, there were great odds that he would win. He could "feel" it.

The increasing noise and clatter of the place told him that soon the morning's drawing would be pulled. With his hands in his pockets and a cigarette slanting across his chin, he stood in the middle of the room and listened to the numbers being called.

"16, 18, 22. . . ."

"45, 68, 50. . . ."

A fat, brown-skinned woman came to him, holding a pad of paper and a pencil.

"What you saying, Jake?"

"Aw, I ain't saying nothing."

"You playing this morning?"

"Maybe. I don't know."

"What you see last night?"

"Aw, Mabel, I saw a hell of a lot. I couldn't half sleep for dreaming, all night long."

"That sounds like money, man."

"I dreamed about steps."

"Steps?"

"Yeah."

"Gee, that sounds good!" said Mabel, turning, holding her paper and pencil ready. "Say, Martha!" she called to an old black woman sitting with a thick book in her hands behind a rickety table. "Say, Martha, what's the Steprow?"

Without looking up, the old woman repeated, "Steprow?" and began to turn the pages of *King Solomon's Wheel of Life and Death Dream Book* with a wet thumb. Then she called:

"Steprow: 6, 17, 26. . . ."

And as the numerical interpretations of Jake's dream were called, Mabel jotted them on to her pad.

"How much you want to play on it?" she asked.

"Make it fourbits," said Jake.

"Aw, come on. Play more than that," said Mabel.

"Make it sixbits then," said Jake, knowing that the more he played the higher her commission would be.

"That's swell," she said. "And what else you dream?"

"Let me see now. . . . You see, I thought I was running up some steps."

"Give me that Runningrow, Martha?" Mabel called.

The old wrinkled thumb turned the dirty leaves.

"Runningrow: 11, 15, 67. . . ."

"You want to play this, too?"

Jake hesitated.

"Listen, Jake," said Mabel, coming close to him. "You just as well play 'em both. Suppose the Runningrow comes out and you done only played the Steprow? You see, you'll be out of luck."

"All right," said Jake. "Give me twobits on that."

"Make it fourbits, Jake."

"All right. Fourbits then."

"And what else you dream?"

"I ain't got no more money," said Jake.

"Now, listen here, Jake, you better play your whole dream if you want to catch something. That's the big trouble with people playing policy; they won't cover a dream. You can never tell what's the really important thing in a dream, so you has to play safe and cover it all to be sure. Now, what else you dream?"

"Well, I thought I was running up some steps and somebody was calling me. You know, I thought it was my boss man on the job."

"That Boss Manrow's lucky. A man just caught it yestiddy." Mabel turned. "Say, Martha, give me that Boss Manrow!"

"Boss Manrow?"

The leaves rustled.

"Boss Manrow: 17, 21, 37. . . ."

"Come on, Jake, and play it. You'll have your whole dream covered, then."

"Give me sixbits on that one, too. And that's all I'm going to play today. I ain't got but fifty cents to get to work and back."

"Honey, if all your numbers come you'll have two hundred dollars," said Mabel.

"Jeeesus," said Jake.

Mabel left him and wandered about the room, looking for other customers. Jake leaned against a wall and listened to the voices calling numbers. *Lawd, if I catch two hundred dollars I won't have to borrow nothing from Jones.*

"Jim, what you dream last night?"

"Man, I dream about snakes."

"Say, Martha, give me that Snakerow!"

"Snakerow? Snakerow: 16, 32, 64. . . ."

"Give me a dime on it. I want to try to catch something to pay my rent."

"Say, Honey, what you dream?"

"Lawd, child, I dreamed about a dead man!"

"A *dead* man?"

44

"Yes, siree! He was laidout right in my room."

"That Deadrow always pulls. You want a gig?"

"I ain't got but three cents."

"Anything with the name of Uncle Sam on it is good around here."

"O.K."

"Say, Martha, what's the Deadrow?"

"Deadrow? Deadrow: 9, 19, 29. . . ."

"You know one thing? I dreamed I saw a ghost last night."

"Ghostrow? Ghostrow: 20, 25, 30. . . ."

"What you dream?"

"Shucks, I dreamed I was pregnant."

"Pregnant?"

"Nothing different!"

Jake laughed and looked at the crowd surrounding the woman, eager to get her number in order to play her dream.

"I ain't never seen that Pregnantrow fail!"

"What's that, Martha?"

"Pregnantrow? Pregnantrow: 11, 22, 50. . . ."

"You better play it!"

"Books are closed! Books are closed!" a heavy voice called.

Jake turned and saw a fat, black man with a cigar in his mouth standing in the door leading to the Wheel.

"Books are closed!" echoed round and round the room.

Activity stopped. The Wheel was brought into the center of the floor; it consisted of a small wooden stand upon which rested a huge lard can. The can held 78 pieces of rubber hose cut to one-inch lengths. In each of these pieces of hose was a curled strip of oil cloth on which numbers had been stamped. A "checker" with a green eyeshade inspected the pieces of hose to see that all was fair. Two hundred pairs of eyes watched eagerly. Finally, it was ascertained to the satisfaction of all present that the 78 numbers were in the 78 pieces of hose.

"All right! Let her go!" the fat, black man called.

"Who wants to pull?"

"I do!"

"Let me pull!"

"Let a lady pull!"

"Naw, let a man pull!"

Jake pushed forward.

"Say, I ain't never pulled!" he called.

"Here's a man what ain't never pulled!"

"Yeah, let 'im pull! He'll be lucky!"

"Come you, if you want to pull!"

The crowd surged around Jake.

45

"Pull my number, partner!"

"Lawd, I hope you pulls something for me!"

Jake was blindfolded with a strip of black silk. The 78 pieces of hose were put into the lard can and shaken vigorously, then the top was eased off slowly so that the numbers would not be disturbed.

"All right, Mister, you can pull now."

Jake reached gropingly into the can. He was trembling. *Jeesus, if I can only pull my numbers!* Slowly and tenderly, he lifted twelve numbers, one after the other, lifted them as though he were lifting nuggets of gold. As he brought forth each piece of hose a "checker" took it and punched out the small bit of oil cloth and called the number.

"Lawd, have mercy! That's the first number of my gig!"

"Mister, please pull something for me!"

"All my numbers but *one!*"

"Lawd, let me catch something, let me catch something . . ."

A man in an inky apron hovered over a rickety machine and set each number into type as it was called. When the first "leg" was completed, the 12 pieces of hose with the bits of oil cloth reinserted were put back into the can with the rest of the numbers and shaken again. Then Jake pulled out 12 more numbers for the second "leg". Two seconds after the drawing stopped the machine clattered and a whirlwind of varicolored slips of paper began to pile up. Jake snatched the cloth from his eyes and grabbed one.

BLACK GOLD

198	A M	182
78		64
75		39
47		13
45		65
38		10
51		26
41		55
26		38
13		17
18		28
73		23
8		73

Sweat stood on his forehead as he compared his numbers with the numbers on the slip. *Let see now. . . . Boss Man-*

*row: 17, 21, 37. . . . Let see. . . . Hunh! Only one num-
ber! 17. . . . Let see about my Runningrow. 11, 15, 67.
. . . Nothing fell. . . . Gawd. . . . Let me see my Steprow now.
Lawd, I ought to catch something somewhere. . . . Hot
dog! Here's 17. . . . And here's my 26, over in the other
leg. . . . And ain't no 6 at all. . . . Ain't that a bitch?* His
lips hung loose and he stared vacantly at the floor. *Gawddamn these sonofabitching numbers!* He crushed the paper
into a tight wad and threw it into a corner. *If I hadn't played
them numbers I would've had two dollars anyhow, now I'm
almost dead broke. . . .* He stumbled out into the sunshine.

He walked slowly, head down, tugging at his collar; he
felt hot and uncomfortable about the neck. It seemed as
though everything was going wrong this morning. *First,
it's Lil and her big mouth. Then it's these Gawddamn numbers! I'll never be fool enough to play them things again!*
He crossed a street and turned north. *Yeah, maybe if I'd
played all the numbers I could get on my dream, I would've
won something.* Yes, he would try that next time. He would
break that policy wheel yet. Just wait. He would win five
hundred dollars, or maybe five thousand, or maybe five hund-
dred thousand. . . . He'd win so much the owner would be
pleading with him to borrow some of it back so he could
pay off his customers. Just wait.

He paused at a corner. *Wonder what Lil's doing now?* His
muscles stiffened and there flashed through his mind a vivid
picture of Lil talking to the milkman. *Yeah, that guy might've
waited till he thought I was gone and slipped back up there.
Maybe they's carrying on now? By Gawd!* His face hardened.
*Yeah, any woman what won't have nothing to do with her
own husband's sure messing with some other man.* He saw
Lil as he had seen her that morning when he had come into
the kitchen; he saw her head thrown back, her eyes closed
with laughter, her shoulders shaking. He whirled and walked
rapidly down an alley, heading toward home. No woman
was going to cheat on him! Not if he could help it! He
reached his alley and hurried down to his back gate. There
was no milk wagon in sight. *Maybe he ain't there? But you
can never tell. If he's there he's got sense enough not to
leave his wagon setting out in the back of my house where I
can see it. The wagon might be around the corner somewhere. And he might be up there right now. . . .* He pulled
up the back steps, taking them four at a time, his breath
coming heavily. Gaining the landing, he crept softly to the
glass panel of his kitchen door and peeped in. He relaxed.
There was Lil, sitting almost as he had left her. She was still
at the breakfast table. Her back was to the door and her
face was buried in her arms. Jake smiled. A copy of *Unity*

was spread with the pages open at her elbow; from where he was standing he could read the large type on the title page:

JESUS SILENTLY HELPS. . . .

He eased back down the steps. *She's all right. But she better not try any tricks on me.* When he reached the street he walked idly, feeling a haunting and hungering sense of incompleteness.

V.

Jake loitered in front of a movie house, looking at lurid posters. In the center of the sidewalk was a huge yellow billboard with purple-bordered placards. A wide strip of green canvas with white letters read:

THE DEATH HAWK
For Three Days Only—See It Now
Tuesday—Wednesday—Thursday
—starring—
JACK BLACKSTONE and GLORIA GOLDENROD
GREATEST OF ALL FLYING PICTURES . . . ACTION . . .
SUSPENSE . . . THRILLS AND STOLEN LOVE

He stepped closer.

The first poster showed

a bluehelmeted aviator in a bloodred monoplane darting shooting speeding zooming careening out of a bank of snow-white clouds in hot pursuit of two green monoplanes and just above the cockpit of the red plane the hero's head could be seen and his eyes were blazing deathly hate and his lips were skinned back over his teeth in a horrible avenging grin and the faces of the two aviators in the fleeing planes were desperate despairing hopeless and at the side of the hero sat a golden-haired blue-eyed girl operating a machinegun spewing fire and death and the girl's hair was blown straight back in the wind and her eyes were widened in fear and

the next poster showed

the hero creeping into a darkened garage on feet of feathers upon a small ratlike creature who had a huge hammer and

48

a gleaming chisel in his hands all raised and he was about to puncture the gas tank of an auto in which the golden-haired girl was seated but behind the hero unsuspected unseen unheard crept a blackbearded giant whose snarling teeth were stained no doubt by whiskey or tobacco juice and who had a huge monkey wrench upraised and ready to swish crash smash heave it down upon the curly head of the innocent hero and

the next poster showed

a group of gangsters who looked like mexicans or japs or reds or huns or just some kind of desperate foreigners and these men were stationed high upon the edge of a sheer cliff overlooking the sea and a rocky coast far below and two of them had the hero's bound tied trussed body upon their shoulders and were about to dash it far below to the rocks and the hero's body was tense taut alert straining against the ropes that held him and instead of looking with horror at the rocks far below which meant death he was gazing with love into the eyes of the golden-haired blue-eyed girl who lay on the ground gagged tied bound trussed and above the girl stood a darkly handsome stranger in a tall silk hat and a winged collar and a frocked coat and in his delicate snowwhite hands which had never worked hard and honestly for a living was a tiny pearlhandled revolver and his slitty black eyes were fastened hard upon the girl's exposed thigh and his red lips were smirking and

the next poster showed

the darkly handsome stranger seated in the dimlit booth of a chinese restaurant with all those funny kind of writings all round the wall you know the kind of writing that looks like a bunch of snakes all trying to bite one another and the golden-haired girl was seated opposite the darkly handsome stranger and she was dabbing her large beautiful sleepy dreamy pale blue eyes with a tiny white handkerchief and the darkly handsome stranger was looking at her with infinite satisfaction as he twirled his waxed mustache and immediately behind the girl's chair partly hidden by thick black curtains unsuspected unseen unheard stood an evileyed slanteyed yellowfaced spoolchinned bonycheeked tightlipped chinkchink chinaman and in his long skinny yellow fingers fingers that had nails that could slit a man's jugular vein and in these fingers was a black vial with the word knockout drops marked plainly and the chinaman was slowly drop-

49

ping black drops into the girl's glass unsuspected unseen unheard and

the next poster showed

the brunette hero having recovered from his death dash into the sea in the process of delivering a fast hard straight sweet true uppercut to the darkly handsome stranger's chin and

the next poster showed

three planes high over mountains and two of the planes were green and one was red and the red plane was sailing free and easy into the clouds with machinegun smoking and the two green planes were enveloped in smoke and flames and were headed earthward in dizzy tailspins and

the last poster showed

the hero and the golden-haired blue-eyed girl seated comfortably in their bloodred monoplane which was zooming like an eagle into rosy afterglow and the hero's hands were resting lightly upon the controls but the girl's arms were about him and their lips were meeting in a blissful kiss. . . .

Jake wagged his head and sighed. If the show had been open he would have gone in, but it did not open until one o'clock and he had to go to work. *That must be a damn good picture. I'd like to see it before it leaves this place. Being a aviator sure must be fun, 'specially when you on top of another plane and can send it spinning down like that.* . . . As he turned away his eyes lingered on the poster where the girl was tied so that her thigh was exposed.

VI.

"If it ain't old Jake Jackson, the big leaguer!"

Jake felt a hard clap on his right shoulder.

"Well, if it ain't old Streamline!" said Jake, shaking hands with a small, yellow, bareheaded man whose coal-black hair was brushed close to his head.

"Lawd, Jake, I ain't seen you since we was in the minor league."

"Yeah, it's been a long time," said Jake.

"How you hitting these days?"

"Oh, soso. I ain't complaining. How's it with you?"

"Can't even see the ball, boy! Tough titty!"

"What's the matter?"

"They just throwing that ball too fast for me, Jake."

"I reckon it's tough for everybody," said Jake.

"Tough ain't no word for it. Man, sometimes I can't even get to the plate."

"Yeah?"

"Look like the game's about over for me if I don't get some work soon. . . ."

"It's really tough."

"I can't hit. All I can do is bunt and run it out. . . ."

"Aw, it's a bitch," said Jake, pursing his lips and looking off.

They were silent for a moment. Jake looked at Streamline's shabby clothes. *He's raggety's a dime mop. . . .* He felt a little sorry for Streamline, but not too sorry. Streamline's slick black hair always irked him, made him envious and uneasy. That was why he was called Streamline, on account of that slick, straight, black hair of his. *And that old stuck-up sonofabitch struts around bareheaded just to show off his slick wool. He thinks he's better than anybody else just 'cause he's yellow. . . .*

"You still playing ball for Uncle Sam, Jake?"

"Yeah," Jake answered dryly. "I'm still going."

"You lucky if you still on somebody's team."

"Well, I don't know about that," said Jake, regaining his sense of superiority and feeling that he could allow something. "When you boil it all down, it's just the same with everybody. Even with my good job I ain't got nothing."

"But when you got a job you on first base," said Streamline.

"Oh, it beats a blank," Jake conceded ruefully, lighting a cigarette.

Streamline shifted restlessly from one foot to the other, watching Jake out of the corner of his eyes.

"Say, Jake, couldn't you be a pinch hitter for a poor guy that's down and out? I hate to ask you, but I ain't eat today. . . ."

"Honest to Gawd, Streamline, I ain't got nothing but carfare to work and back. I just got through paying the milkman. . . ."

"That's all right," said Streamline hastily. "It's a damn tough game."

"If I had it, I'd let you have it. You know I would. . . ."

"Sure, sure. . . . You always played ball."

They were silent again. Jake gazed down to the corner where the traffic lights flashed from green to red, and back to green again. He spat carefully into the gutter.

"Swell day."

51

"Yeah, it'll be time for baseball pretty soon."

"You get tired of staying cooped up in the house all the time."

"Say, wasn't that too bad about old Mussellinni going over into Ethiopia and knocking old Haile Salassie for a homerun?"

"Wasn't it, though?" answered Jake.

"And Jeeesus, old Joe Louis losing to Schmeling."

"Boy, that made me sick," said Jake.

"You know," said Streamline seriously, "it looks like we black folks is just about to be shutout. We done got two outs on us in the ninth inning. Old Haile Salassie and Joe Louis *both* done struck out!"

"Seems that way," said Jake, wagging his head.

"Well, I'm moving on and see if I can't steal a base on somebody," said Streamline, laughing uneasily.

"See you later."

"So long."

VII.

In the middle of the block Jake saw coming toward him a young black girl whose little firm breasts shook with each step she took. He stared hard and unblinkingly at the gentle sway of her buttocks until she turned a corner. Another woman passed and he could see the prints of her breasts even through the spring coat she wore. He looked at the storefronts to see where he was. *Doc's place is along here somewhere. Yeah, there it is, down the street a bit.* He walked toward a barberpole that revolved in the sunshine like a bright stick of peppermint candy. Above the pole swung a sign.

DOC HIGGINS' TONSORIAL PALACE

He pressed his face against the glass and looked inside. The shop was crowded with a mass of waving arms and flashing teeth and twisted black faces. *What in the world's going on in there?* He pushed into the doorway, sniffing odors of hair lotion and lather. A whirlwind argument was raging; everybody was screaming at once, contending for the right to speak by trying to drown out the other's voice. He edged in as far as he could and then tiptoed to get a look. In the center of the crowd five black faces were yelling at one another. He caught a glimpse of Doc Higgins, his small, fat mouth opening and shutting rapidly, his head bobbing back and forth as though his neck were made of rubber. At the end of each sentence Doc's head would jerk violently backward, making his white goatee and white hair tremble. His voice was far heavier than all the rest, and he finally took the floor by sheer lungpower, pounding his chubby fist into his fat palm. *Yeah, this is good! Old Doc's setting on somebody!*

"Nigger, is you a plumb fool?" screamed Doc.

"Wait, let me tell you something, Doc," pleaded Duke, a skinny black man with a sharp face.

"You can't tell me nothing," shouted Doc Higgins.

"Listen to me a minute, will you, Doc!"

"Listen to you for what?"

"I want to tell you something."

"How come I got to listen to a little snot like you?"

"If you'll just listen I'll tell you a lot you ought to know!"

"Like hell you will!"

The crowd surged, pushing one another.

"Let 'im talk, Doc!"

"Give 'im a chance, Doc!"

"What's the matter, you scared, Doc?"

Doc whirled, his eyes blazing.

"I ain't scared of nothing that's born of woman!"

"Let me talk, then," asked Duke.

Doc took a swift step backwards and swept Duke with his eyes from his head to his feet.

"What you know about life?"

"All due respect to your white hair, I knows a lot more than you."

"Listen, boy," said Doc, mildly and compassionately, "I was kicking and scratching in this old world before you were knee-high to a grasshopper. . . ."

"Aw, Doc, let Duke talk!"

"He's scared," said Duke.

"Naw, I ain't scared. I just ain't going to let no dirty little sneaking Commoonist come in here and tell me what to do with my money! Get out and make your own money, like I did!"

Everybody shouted and Jake edged closer. The argument had him keyed to a high pitch. He was itching to get into it. He could handle guys like Duke. *Just let me get at 'im!* Each time Doc spoke he followed the movements of Doc's lips with his own and nodded approval.

"Where can a man get a job?" Duke screamed.

"You don't want no job!" Doc bawled.

"That's a lie and you know it!"

"Aw, Duke, I know your kind inside and out!"

"Answer his question, Doc. He asked you where can a man get a job!"

"I ain't suppose to tell 'im," said Doc.

"We ain't the only ones who's out of work," said Duke. "So what?"

"Times ain't like they was when you was young, Doc."

"So what?"

"How can a man get a job when there ain't none?"

"Make your own job like I did!"

"Doc, you can't see facts! You blind!"

"Aw, you niggers full of crap!"

Doc whirled around and bumped into Jake.

" 'Lo, Jake." He grabbed Jake's shoulder and turned again to Duke. "Here's a sensible young man with a good, steady job. Here's somebody your own age. Ask 'im something. Say, Jake, tell this loudmouthed Know Nothing something!"

Jake smiled and looked down at the keen creases in his trousers. Duke eyed him sullenly.

"How many before me, Doc?" asked Jake, ignoring him.

"You next."

When Jake pulled off his coat and vest his government badge glittered on his suspenders. Doc pointed to it.

"See that, Duke?"

"Yeah. What about it?"

"This man's with Uncle Sam, win, lose, or draw."

"He's losing," said Duke.

"Like hell I is!" snapped Jake. "What you think you going to do, overthrow the government?"

"If we have to, yes."

Jake laughed, without smiling, mirthlessly.

"Nigger, you'd last as long trying to overthrow the government as a fart in a wind storm!"

Doc grabbed the back of the barberchair and let out a high, whinnying laugh.

"I ain't alone," said Duke stubbornly. "There's millions like me. Maybe not in this country yet, but over in Russia. . . ."

"There he goes!" said Jake. "If you talk to a crackbrain two minutes he'll start slobbering about Roosia! Why can't you *red* niggers get some sense in your heads? Don't you know them Reds is just using you? When they get tired of you they throw you away like a dirty sock! Look at the Doc here! He's a race man! A precinct captain. A businessman. A property owner. He's got pull with all the big politicians down in the Loop. And here you, raggety and dirty, going around talking about overthrowing the government. Doc's setting pretty; why don't you play the game? What you belly-aching about?"

54

"Gawddamn right I'm setting pretty," mumbled Doc, stropping his razor. "And I'm going to stay that way."

"You guys just wait and see," said Duke. "A few of you guys got something, but most of the black people in this country ain't got nothing. All them sharecroppers. . . ."

"To hell with them!" said Jake. "Let 'em look out after themselves!"

"But they ain't got nothing to eat," insisted Duke.

"Is you hungry?" asked Jake, taking a dime out of his pocket.

"Naw," said Duke.

"Well, what you squawking about?"

"There's thousands of people starving. . . ."

"Is we the cause of that?" asked Doc.

"Naw, but it don't make no difference. . . ."

"Listen Duke," said Doc, slipping his arm around Duke's shoulders. "Let me tell you a story. Once upon a time there was a little frog. Somebody threw that frog into a churn of milk. Now that frog kicked and kicked and kicked and tried to get out. After awhile he saw little pieces of yellow butter coming, like little pieces of gold, see? Well, the frog kept kicking and kicking and all that butter came together into one great big yellow ball. Then, you know what that frog did? He jumped on top of that ball of butter and hopped right out of the churn. . . ." Doc paused and pulled from his pocket a thick roll of green bills. "You see this?"

"Yeah," mumbled Duke.

"You know what this is?"

"It's money. . . ."

"Naw, fool! It's butter!"

Jake bent to the floor and slapped his thigh. Doc held the roll of bills for awhile under Duke's nose, then rammed it back into his pocket, and let out a long laugh. The crowd began to file slowly out, making wry faces at one another.

"Go get some butter, you chumps!" yelled Jake.

"You guys just wait," threatened Duke.

"You talk like a fool," said Doc.

"Two fools," said Jake.

Duke filed out with the rest and slammed the door.

"Did you ever see such a nutty bastard?" asked Doc, tucking the white cloth around Jake's neck.

"Doc," said Jake. "Niggers is just like a bunch of crawfish in a bucket. When one of 'em gets smart and tries to climb out of the bucket, the others'll grab hold on 'im and pull 'im back. . . ."

"Ain't it the truth? What can you do with such a fool?"

"He'll wake up some day," said Jake.

They were silent a moment. Doc combed Jake's hair, preparatory to cutting it.

"Well, what you know, Jake?"

"I'm having trouble with that bitch of mine."

"Yeah, what seems to be the matter?"

"Aw, she's sick again."

"What's the trouble this time?"

"She's gone and got herself a tumor."

"A tumor?"

"Yeah."

"Gee, man, that's serious," said Doc, shaking his head sympathetically.

"Now she's got to be operated on."

"Damn, that's tough."

"It's going to cost me five hundred bucks."

Doc took a huge chew of tobacco and spat a long brown stream into a spittoon.

"She's sticking you up aplenty. . . ."

"But that ain't half of it."

"What's happened?"

"Aw, I had to slap her a few times this morning."

"That's bad. She might report you."

"Yeah, that's just what I'm scared of."

"You know the government's pretty hard on you now for things like that."

"That's what I want to talk with you about."

"O.K. Shoot."

"You know I've been up before that Board twice."

"Yeah, and they ain't standing for no foolishness now. They know times is bad and they can always get men to work."

"You still got some pull with the Post Master, ain't you?"

"Well, in a way."

"I want you to put in a good word for me, Doc."

"Well, Jake, I'm telling you. So much has been going on lately, it's sort of hard to get at them guys unless—"

"Unless what?"

"Well, you have to make them guys want to talk to you. You see, I have to go through four or five men now to get to the Post Master. And them guys want money."

"What do you think it'll cost?"

"It'll cost you a hundred dollars, Jake."

"Jeeesus, Doc!"

"Aw, I know it's tough, Jake. But that's the way the land lays these days. . . ."

"But, Doc, I got to pay out five hundred for that operation."

They were silent. Doc was now cutting Jake's hair with the

clippers. *Buzzzzzzzzz.* . . . The big clock on the wall went *ticktock . . . ticktock . . . ticktock.* . . . Jake lit a cigarette and spat a shred of tobacco. Doc laid his hand on Jake's shoulder.

"Well, Jake, I'll tell you. Since it's you, and since you're a friend of mine, I'll do the job for seventy-five."

"You can't do no better?"

"Not a cent."

"Well, how soon can you get to the Post Master?"

"When can you give me something?"

"Payday."

"How much?"

"Maybe I can squeeze out a five-dollar payment. . . ."

"O.K. Since it's you, Jake, I'll do it."

"That's swell, Doc. Gee, that sure takes a big load off my chest. If she done been down I'll 'phone you, and tell 'em, Doc, that that woman of mine is just nuts, see? Tell 'em I'm doing all I can."

"Just leave it to me. I'll fix it up."

The clippers went *buzzzzzzzzzzz.* . . . Jake took a last draw from his cigarette and flicked it into the spittoon.

"You know, Jake, some niggers is sure funny."

"What's that?"

"I was just thinking about Duke."

"Aw," said Jake, waving his hand. "Them kind of niggers is crazy!"

"But what we going to do with 'em?"

"Say, don't you worry. If they tie up with them Reds and start anything, the white folks'll take care of 'em good and plenty."

"You know one thing?"

"What's that?"

"Niggers talk too much."

"Nothing hurts a duck but his bill."

"If they kept their damn mouths shut and tried to get hold of something, some money, or property, then they'd get somewhere."

"Sure. Now, what would I do in my case if it wasn't for men like you who's done something and can help me?"

"That's right."

"Aw, them niggers ought to be taken out and shot."

"Shooting's too good for 'em."

They were silent again. Doc was now trimming Jake's hair with the shears. *Clip . . . clip . . . clip . . . clip.* . . . Doc spat the long brown stream into the spittoon.

"Swell weather we're having."

"You bet."

"Feel's like spring's done come."

"Yeah; and it feels good, too."

"Makes a man feel young again."

"That ain't no lie."

Jake looked out of the window at the traffic moving by. He began to hum a tune and swing his feet gently. Then, for some inexplicable reason, he stopped humming and began to whistle softly. With a look of boredom, he stopped whistling and watched the reflection of Doc in the mirror. He followed the shining glint of the shears as they rose and fell. Sighing, he looked out of the window again. Like a scrap of paper blown by wind, his attention wandered. He looked at the ceiling. At the floor. Then at the flyspecked electric globe that burned above his head. His eyes finally rested on a faded calendar. For the want of something better to do he spelled out the words slowly in a low breath:

GUARANTEED INSURANCE

He frowned. Sighed. Crossed his legs. Lit another cigarette. Drummed his fingers on the arm of the chair.

"Say, Jake?"

"Yeah?"

"You see in the papers where old lady Lucy Rosenball donated a million dollars to the colored folks for a college down South?"

"Yeah, I was reading about that. That was swell."

"Wasn't it, though?"

"That means the colored people's making progress."

"You bet."

"You know, she sure is a nice old lady."

"Yeah. The paper said she's done donated about five million to build a hospital for stray cats and dogs."

"Now you know she must got a kind heart."

"Yeah, some white folks is good, that way."

"You know, I always said that we colored folks ought to stick with the rich white folks. . . ."

"That's the only way we'll ever get anywhere."

"Ain't that what old Booker Washington said? Cooperate and get along?"

"That's right."

"That's what Duke ought to think about instead of running around here talking about overthrowing the government."

"Aw, he's crazy!"

"Wonder what in the world can be wrong with some folks' brains?"

"Just dumb, that's all. Just plain dumb."

As the shears clipped about Jake's neck he sighed, and

lazily shifted his weight from one buttock to the other. The continual clipping made him drowsy.

"Just a minute," said Doc. "I want to turn on the radio."

"O.K."

The radio poured forth a volume of martial music; the music stopped and a man spoke:

> . . . The mystic chords of memory, stretching from every battlefield and patriot grave to every living heart and hearthstone all over this broad land, will yet swell the chorus of the Union when again touched, as they surely will be, by the better angels of our nature. . . .

"What's that?" asked Doc.

"What?"

"That on the radio. A speech or something?"

"Aw, naw. Just something about the Civil War," said Jake, yawning.

"Civil War?"

"Yeah. This is old Abe Lincoln's Birthday, you know."

"Oh."

> . . . Let us forget ourselves and join hands, like brothers, to save the Republic. If we succeed, there will be glory enough for all. . . .

Jake listened awhile and was soon sleeping again. He tilted forward.

"Hold up!"

"Hunh?"

"Set up straight, man."

Jake straightened, shook his head and sucked back loose saliva. The shears when *clip . . . clip . . . clip . . . clip. . . .* The clipping and the radio made Jake doze again. Doc spat his long brown stream.

"Say, Jake?"

"Yeah?"

"That Civil War sure was some war, wasn't it?"

"You bet your sweet life it was," said Jake, belching.

"And a lot of guys was killed in that war, too."

"War's a bad thing."

"Oh, yeah. War's bad all right."

"And old Abe Lincoln sure was a smart man."

"A *great* man."

"He was what I call a man of Gawd," said Doc in a deep, bass voice.

"He couldn't've done what he done if he didn't have Gawd with 'im," said Jake.

59

"You got to take Gawd with you."

"Yeah, because you can't do nothing without 'Im."

"You know, that makes me think of a good old Christian woman I used to know," began Doc. "She was a widow with nine children on her hands. And man, you know one thing, that woman raised all nine of them children and not a one of them was ever in a jail."

"Gawd sure must have been with her," said Jake, wagging his head in admiration.

"You *know* He was!"

"He's the only one what can guide you through such tough days as that."

"The only one."

"You know, I heard about a soljer that went through the war wearing a Bible right next to his heart. He went all through the war and come out without a *scratch*."

"See what *faith* can do!"

"Folks in the old days use to work miracles."

"Jesus walked on water, you know."

"It's all in how much faith you got."

"Yeah, faith's the main thing."

"Faith can move mountains."

Doc's mouth became full of spit and he could not talk. The shears went *clip . . . clip . . . clip . . . clip. . . .* Jake's head tilted.

"Hold up Jake."

"Oh, Lawd! Man, I'm sleepy's hell!"

. . . President Lincoln issued a call for volunteers. The response was overwhelming in its generosity and intensity. The miners, the farmers, and workers of all trades dropped their tools and swarmed into the ranks of the Union Armies. . . .

"O.K."

"You through?"

"Yeah."

Jake got down and stretched.

"What's the damages, Doc?"

"Four bits."

Jake paid, giving fifteen cents for a tip.

"Thanks. Come in soon."

"O.K. And don't forget what I told you about my wife."

"Oh, naw. I'll telephone right down when you get in touch with me."

Jake put on his hat and coat.

"See you later, Old Timer."

"So long, Big Shot."

As he went through the door the radio sang:

. . . John Brown's body lies amouldering in the grave,
His soul goes marching on. . . .

VIII.

Jake stood on the corner of 47th Street and Forestville Avenue. Sunshine was spread everywhere and the intense light hurt his eyes. His arms and legs felt heavy and slightly numb, as though they were watersoaked. He licked his lips, mumbling, *Gawd, but I'm sleepy.* If he could only sleep right now, if he could only close his eyes and rest his head upon something soft. There was in the air a faint, sweet smell, a tantalizing presage of spring. A slow restlessness made him wriggle his toes in his shoes. He had a longing to see green grass, to go into the park and stretch out flat on his back with his face to the sky. He fumbled in his vest pocket for a match, split it with a thumbnail, and dug at a cavity in a back tooth. He took out his watch; it was nine o'clock. He had a full three hours before worktime. He leaned against a steel telephone post and let the match dangle loosely from his lips. He wanted to go somewhere, but he could not think of a suitable place. Above all, he did not want to go home; he was in no mood to argue with Lil now. *But that bitch better watch her step.* He looked at the pavement; something cold seemed to come over him. *Yeah, I been too easy with her. I got to crack down; I been letting her have her way too long.* Two thin spirals of smoke eddied from his nostrils into sunshine. He squinted his eyes, feeling lazy and restless and a little sad. He wanted something, and that something hungered in him, deeply. He went into a drugstore, bought a package of cigarettes, and walked west on 47th Street to his favorite poolroom, the *SidePocket Billiard Nook*; but he did not go in. The noise emanating from the half-opened doorway told him that he was not in a mood for the antics of the old gang. But where could he go? He wondered if his pal, Bob, were up. *Dammit, that's the big trouble with Bob; he always sleeps so late.* Well, he had to kill some time; he turned on to South Parkway and went south, swinging his body importantly. About him traffic roared and horns honked. People came and went; each seemed to have a definite destination. Their hurry made him hurry. He turned to his right and walked up 48th Street. He was going to Bob's, but, really, he did not want

61

to go to Bob's. He wanted to go somewhere else; he thought of a certain apartment and a certain woman. He looked at his watch again; it was five minutes past nine. *Yeah, that's the big trouble with working part of the day and part of the night. When you's off there ain't no place to go.* He paused at 48th Street and Michigan Avenue, in front of the George Cleveland Hall Branch of the Chicago Public· Library. People were going in and out. Across the door a sign read:

LIBRARY CLOSED—LEGAL HOLIDAY
Only Reference Rooms Open

He studied the building with curiosity. *That's right. I ain't never looked around in one of them joints.* The rows upon rows of dull-colored books struck him as being peculiarly odd. They seemed somehow funny, something like a game, or like the little dolls in a shooting gallery. He tiptoed and saw many people bent over desks. *I wonder what they charge you to go in there?* He had long planned to visit one of these places, but it had always happened that he could never get around to it. *I'd just like to go in and look around, like I done that time me and Lil went to the Field Museum.* But not today. *Naw, naw, not today.* He would go some other time when he had lots of time; that would be better. Some Saturday afternoon when he was off and did not have anything else to do. *Yeah, it would be a damn good idea to come here for a picnic someday, bring a nice big lunch and stay around all day. Then I can tell old Bob and Al and Slim all about the big books I seen and they'll be jealous as hell. . . .*
He walked toward 47th Street again, and near the end of the block he saw a black boy sitting in a window reading a book. He shook his head. *Too much reading's bad.* It was all right to read the newspapers, and things like that; but reading a lot of books with fine print in them and no pictures would drive you crazy. Especially young people. His mind went back to his boyhood; he remembered a schoolmate of his who had become queer from trying to memorize the Bible. *Yeah, too much reading's bad. It addles your brains, and if you addle your brains you'll sure have bookworms in the brain.* His poor old grandmother had told him that when he was a child, and he had never forgotten it, and had never had bookworms. But it was all right if you were studying for the pulpit. *Oh, yeah; that's different. Gawd's angels'll watch over you then and keep you from going crazy.* And anyhow, making folks crazy was God's way with those who wanted to know too much. Many are called and few are chosen. He had never been chosen.

62

When he reached Bob's place he stood on the sidewalk, smoking, and could not make up his mind. Well, he might as well. He had nothing else to do. He went into the vestibule, rang the bell, and in answer to a buzzer, climbed to the third apartment. Bob, a man as black as himself, stood holding the door.

"Think about the Devil and he comes!"

"Who you calling a Devil?"

"You, you rascal!"

"How you today, Bob?"

"Soso. How's yourself?"

"Aw, pretty good. What you know?"

"Nothing. Same old 6's and 7's. What you know?"

"Nothing, man. I was just passing and thought I'd drop in."

"I'm glad you come. I was just setting here wishing somebody'd come along."

"If Al and Slim'd come over we could have a good game of bridge."

"Yeah, Lawd. Set down."

"O.K."

"Smoke?"

"Naw, got some."

They lit cigarettes and puffed awhile silently.

"How's the weather out?"

"Swell. Feels like spring."

"I sure wish summer'd hurry up and come on."

"Yeah, give me summer any day."

"Me too, boy."

"But we got a lot of cold weather coming yet."

"Oh, no doubt of that."

"March'll bring a lot of cold blizzards."

"And April a lot of sleet and rain."

"Yeah, we got a lot of cold weather coming yet."

"Oh, yeah."

Bob coughed up something into his mouth and swallowed it.

"Say, what we doing tonight?" he asked.

"How about this new place I was telling you about?"

"Where is it?"

"Over on Calumet."

"Who runs it?"

"Aw, some dame named Rose. They got gambling, women. . . ."

"That suits me."

"But I'm broke."

"Same here."

"Say, if I can get a loan from old Jones today, will you sign for me?"

"Sure."

"I tried to catch some policy this morning, but didn't have no luck."

"Aw, them numbers ain't no good."

Jake leaned back in his chair and yawned.

"I ssssure dddonnnnnnnn't feeeel like wwwworking to-day. . . ."

"Me neither."

"Feels sort of lowdown."

"Gee, I hate to have that feeling come down on me."

"That old lazy, blue feeling. . . ."

"If I had some dough we could go to that flat we was at last Tuesday."

"Jeeeeesus!"

They looked at each other and grinned.

"Say?" asked Jake.

"Hunh?"

"Got anything on your hip?"

"Sure, want a little nip?"

"Yeah, I'm in the dumps."

"O.K."

Bob left for the interior of the flat and came back with a small glass and an amber-colored flask.

"Help yourself."

"Naw, you pour it."

Bob poured the glass full.

"Ain't you drinking?" asked Jake.

"Naw, I'm on the wagon."

"Aw, man, come on. Ain't no fun this way."

"Naw, I tell you."

"What's the matter?"

"Aw. . . ."

Bob half turned and waved his hand disgustedly.

"What's eating you?"

"It's down on me again, Jake."

"You let a little thing like that keep you from drinking?"

"It's running, Jake. The doctor said. . . ."

"Aw, hell!"

Jake tossed the whiskey down his throat, then sat looking at Bob with a pitying smile.

"Listen, Bob, that ain't no worse'n a bad cold. That doctor don't know what he's talking about. I had it. A man ain't a man unless he's done had it. Come on and drink."

"Naw, the last time I got drunk I nearly died."

"You ain't no good."

"Humph!" grunted Bob. "Man, you don't *know*. This

thing's a bitch! I been around here feeling like I wanted to go out every hour and pull up trees by their roots!"

"Who you catch it from?"

"I wish I could find the bitch!"

"Gee, nigger, you in a helluva fix. Your wife riding you for alimony, and you got a dose."

"It's hell," said Bob, sitting down and stretching out his legs.

"Well," said Jake. "You ain't no worse off'n me."

"How's that?"

Jake told Bob of Lil, of how Doc had promised to help him, and of how much he owed.

"Hell, you lucky and don't know it," said Bob.

"You nuts!"

"Listen, long as that old wife stays single, I got to pay that twenty bucks a week alimony for her and them kids. On top of that I got my own expenses. And on top of that, I got this damn dose. Some times I think I'm going nuts, no kidding. . . . It's hell when you have to set in your room, knowing even if you went out you can't do nothing. You know, I never knowed what a woman meant till this thing got so bad on me. I just set here and feel like running and jumping straight through that stone wall."

"You ain't no good," said Jake, taking another drink. "Ain't you really going to take just one? . . . One won't hurt you."

"Not so you can notice it."

"The trouble with you is, you was too easy on your wife," Jake said meditatively. "You ought to seen me bearing down on old Lil this morning."

"Yeah, I wish I had beat her now," said Bob. "She lied to the judge and told 'im I beat her anyhow."

"See? Either you trick them or they'll trick you."

"I reckon you right. I know if I had it to go through with again I'd sure do different. And just think. . . ." Bob stood up, his lips flexing. "Just think that old bitch told the judge I was running around with other women, and what was *she* doing?"

"They all that way, Bob."

"She made me pay the court costs and I believe my soul there was something between her and that lawyer. One of these days I'm going to get good and mad and throw up everything. Sometimes I feel like quitting my job just to get even with her."

"Yeah, but ain't no use of cutting off your nose to spite your face."

Bob smote his fist in his palm, sighed, and sat down again.

65

"Uuuuuunmp! This is good stuff," said Jake, licking his lips. "Hell, Bob, take a little, just a little."

"I tell you I ain't drinking. I can't forget last time. Honest to Gawd, I felt like taking that Tribune Tower and turning it bottomside upwards a hundred times a day."

They were silent. Steam hissed in the radiator. Jake belched and nestled his head deep into a corner of the sofa. He was pleasantly vacuous; he could hear the faint noises in the street below and now and then, the dull rumble of the faraway "L". He crossed his legs, uncrossed them, sat up straight for about five seconds, leaned over a second, then sat up straight again.

"Gawd, I wish Al and Slim would come on."

"Me too."

"We could have a game then."

"Don't time pass slow?"

"Don't it?"

"Just drags."

"Makes you nervous."

" 'Specially when you ain't got nothing to do."

"I never did like to just *set*."

"Me neither."

"Yeah, it gets on your nerves."

Jake took another drink.

"Say, ain't it too bad about Slim?"

"Jake, he's a sick man."

"You reckon. . . ."

"He's getting worst."

"That guy ought to go west for his T.B."

"If he stays around here he's making a date with the undertaker."

"The Post Office ain't no place for a man with consumption."

"You telling me?"

"He was so weak the other day he had to check out and go home."

"Was that the reason why he left?"

"Sure. He was about to drop."

"Yeah, his eyes is always feverish."

"He keeps a fever around a hundred all the time."

"Jeeesus!"

"You know, it goes all through me just to hear that guy cough."

"Yeah, seems like his insides is coming up."

"And he drinks too damn much."

"Maybe he wants to keep from worrying."

"Maybe so."

66

"Hell, he ain't got but a few more years. He just as well get something out of life. You don't live but once."

"Shucks, Bob, you got it easy, compared with him."

"Yeah, I reckon I'm lucky after all."

"Ain't it funny about folks what's got T.B. They a hound for women. . . ."

"Yeah, looks like Slim just can't get enough."

"Lawd, that guy sure loves his meat."

"He's a hound dog from way back yonder."

"Looks like T.B. just drives 'em to it."

"Yeah, old Slim just can't help himself."

"He's a good old fellow, though."

"They don't make 'em any better'n Slim."

"Yeah, he's a brick."

"Ain't it funny how two guys like Slim and Al can be so different?"

"Ain't it, though? Al's a mess! That nigger thinks he's a big shot."

"He's a sarjant in the National Guard now."

"For *real*?"

"Sure. He got a drag with the Colonel."

"He's always bragging about what a great soljer he is."

"But he's the toughest nigger I ever seen."

"He don't never get tired."

"He ain't got sense enough to get tired."

"And can eat! Lawd!"

"Al says he's going to get what he can out of this world 'cause he don't live but once."

"Maybe he's right."

"Maybe so."

"Lawd, but I ain't never seen a nigger stingy's he is."

"He says he saving his money to be a bigtime politician."

"That nigger tried to make a political speech during the elections. He got up in a church and forgot what he was going to say. Did the people laugh? . . ."

"He says he's going to open up a beer tavern next year."

"He's always going to *do* something."

"You know one thing, we here laughing at old Al, but that nigger is just dumb enough to turn out to be something, sure enough."

"Yeah, you never can tell."

"A lot of folks who ain't nothing turn out to be something, sometimes."

The door bell rang.

"That maybe Al or Slim now," said Bob, rising and going into the hall.

"How you, mugs!" a deep, bass voice boomed from down the stairs.

"It's Al," Bob hollered to Jake.

"Tell 'im to come on up!" said Jake.

Al, fat, black, filled the doorway with a yellow chinchilla coat. He was puffing, pursing his lips and walling his eyes.

"Lawd, to come up them steps of yours just about kills a man!"

"Aw, come on," said Jake. "You can stand it. You a soljer, ain't you?"

"When you drag two hundred and fifty pounds up three floors, you done done something, if you ask me." He threw his coat and hat over on a sofa, then turned and looked searchingly at Jake and Bob. "What's wrong with you two guys? You look like a couple of sick hens."

"Nothing wrong with me," said Jake.

"Like hell there ain't," said Al gruffly. "I was just by Doc's getting a shave and he told me."

"Well, ain't that enough to be droopy about?" asked Jake.

"And what's wrong with you?" asked Al, turning to Bob.

"Same old thing."

"What's eating you guys? Snap out of it! Don't let that stuff worry you!"

"Al, you the funniest guy!" said Jake. "Don't you never worry?"

"Worry for what?"

"About things?"

"Hell, naw!"

"Not even about that yellow gal who left you?"

"I can get another one just like the other one," said Al. "They all feel alike in the dark."

"You just like a piece of iron," mumbled Bob.

"How you do it, Al?" asked Jake.

"Join the National Guard and find out," said Al.

"I want to ask you something, Al."

"Shoot."

"What you eat for breakfast this morning?"

Al pushed back his coat and hat on the sofa and stretched out, his face turned ceilingward. He puffed a few moments; trying to get his breath.

"Let's see now. . . . I ate half a loaf of bread, all toasted golden brown and buttered. I reckon, I ain't sure now, but I reckon I ate about ten scrambled eggs; it might've been more. And a pound of bacon dripping with good old grease. And a pot of coffee. And some plum preserves. I had a apple on my way here, and I'm hungry now."

"Good Gawd!"

"Nigger, how come you eat that way?"

" 'Cause I like to."

"No wonder you don't never worry."

"I'm going to be eating when I die," said Al.

"Have a drink," said Bob. "You, too, Jake."

They poured drinks.

"Bob ain't drinking," said Jake to Al. "He's running."

"You bad as a little baby," said Al.

"Now if Slim would come we could have that game," said Jake.

"Yeah, I feel like bridge this morning," said Al.

"It wouldn't be bad," said Bob, rising. "I'll be back in a moment."

Al and Jake laughed.

"Don't turn over the house, now!"

"I'm going home," said Jake jokingly. "You might come running out of that bathroom and want to choke us to death."

"You guys wait till you get a dose, then you'll see it ain't nothing to laugh about."

"Aw, you just ain't no good."

When Bob was gone, Al and Jake emptied the flask.

"You know," said Al, licking his lips, "a guy in New York done sent a man here to open a church down on Michigan. The guy says he's Gawd."

"Gawd?" asked Jake, straightening.

"Yeah; he calls hisself Father Divine."

"What's wrong with 'im?"

"I don't know. All I know is, he sent a disciple here and folks is over there praying to 'im."

"Jeesus Christ," said Jake. "Do they sure enough believe 'im?"

"They must to, they pray to 'im."

"What he tell 'em to fool 'em that way?"

"He tells 'em to drop everything and follow him."

Bob came back, bringing another bottle of whiskey.

"Here, help yourself. . . . Say, who's that say they Gawd?"

"A guy in New York."

"A nigger?"

"Sure, he's black as the Ace of Spades."

"And what the white folks say about it?"

"Lots of 'em believing 'im. They say he's got ten thousand folks following 'im."

"You say *white* folks?"

"Sure, it was in the papers."

Bob let out a long, loud laugh.

"Don't laugh, nigger," said Al. "How you know? He might really be Gawd."

"Is you done gone nuts, too?" asked Bob.

"Well, how you know he *ain't* Gawd?" asked Al.

"You know, Gawd did say He was coming again," said Jake.

"And this might be Him," said Al.

"If He is coming, He ain't coming back in no nigger skin," said Bob.

"How come He ain't? He was born in a manger the last time."

"You can't tell what Gawd'll do," said Jake.

"They say there's a lot of proof that he is Gawd," said Al.

"What proof?"

"Well, for one thing the Bible says that Gawd's Church is going to be built on a rock that the very gates of hell can't go against. . . ."

"Yeah. . . ."

"Well, this Father Divine's done built his church on Manhattan Island. Ain't that a rock?"

They were silent, thinking.

"Yeah, folks say it's a rock. . . ."

"It's a rock all right, but. . . ."

"And he heals folks," said Al.

"Well," said Jake. "I ain't saying he is Gawd, and I ain't saying he ain't Gawd."

"Yeah," said Al, warming to his subject. "All the folks hates us black people, so Gawd might have done made up His mind to show 'em that everybody's equal in His sight. So He might come down in a black skin, see? He come as a Jew the last time, and how come He won't come as nigger now? You see, He'd fool all the white folks then."

"Boy!" said Bob, "if that guy *was* Gawd, wouldn't the white folks just die!"

They laughed. The door bell rang.

"I bet that's Slim!"

Slim, tall, brown, thin-faced, came through the door, coughing a little jerky cough. His eyes were bright and hard and he seemed in high spirits. He moved across the room quickly and threw his coat and hat on the sofa.

"What you niggers doing?" he asked.

"Waiting for you so we could play a game of bridge," said Jake.

Slim looked at Al.

"You want to take 'em on this morning?"

"*Them* lambs? Hell, yeah!" said Al.

"Wait a minute. I'll get a table and some cards and we'll see *who's* lambs!" said Bob.

"Calling us *lambs*," sneered Jake, after Bob had gone.

"You can't play no bridge," said Al.

"We beat you last Tuesday," said Slim.

70

"And didn't we beat you last Saturday?"

"Aw, we done beat you guys more times than a man can remember."

"Listen at that nigger lie!" said Al.

Bob came back, set up the card table, and arranged the chairs. They sat. Bob took the deck and commenced shuffling.

"Look at this nigger, will you?" asked Al, turning to Slim.

"What?" asked Bob, innocently.

"Now, ain't this a *dog*!"

"Nigger, what you talking about?" asked Bob.

"Is you just going to *take* the deal?" asked Al.

"You full of stuff!" said Bob, continuing to shuffle the cards.

"Stuff my ass! Let's cut for this deal!"

Bob paused.

"What you trying to signify?"

"Signify hell!" exclaimed Al, clamping his hand over the deck. "Ain't we going to cut for this deal?"

"Take your hands off the cards!" said Jake to Al. "You want me to sock you in your fat puss!"

Al stood up, took a step backward, placed his hands on his hips, and glared.

"Now, ain't this a bitch!" he said.

"I'll sock you so hard your ancestors'll feel it," said Jake.

"And I'll be the last man you'll ever sock!" said Al, leaning forward.

Slim stood up and banged his black fist on the table.

"We's going to cut for this deal, or there ain't going to be no deal!" he said. "What you niggers think we is, anyhow? Think we's just going to *give* you the deal? This ain't no charity station. . . ."

"Aw, dry up!" said Bob, throwing the deck on the table. "We can all cut. . . ."

"Damn right!" said Al.

Bob cut an ace.

"I thought it was going to be my deal," he said.

"Aw, nigger, shut up and deal the cards!" said Al.

"I was doing that," said Bob coolly.

Jake lost patience and pushed his chair back, yelling:

"You niggers keep your shirts on!"

"Here she comes!" said Bob dealing.

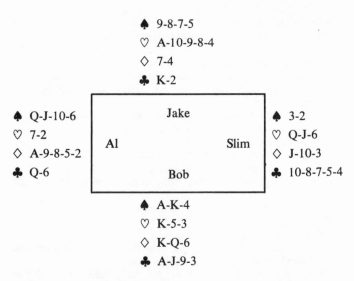

♠ 9-8-7-5
♥ A-10-9-8-4
♦ 7-4
♣ K-2

♠ Q-J-10-6
♥ 7-2
♦ A-9-8-5-2
♣ Q-6

Jake

Al   Slim

Bob

♠ 3-2
♥ Q-J-6
♦ J-10-3
♣ 10-8-7-5-4

♠ A-K-4
♥ K-5-3
♦ K-Q-6
♣ A-J-9-3

They were silent, examining and sorting their hands. Finally, Al looked up, tapped the table with his cards, and said to Bob:

"Wake up and say what you going to do!"

Bob frowned and slouched deeper into his chair. He was trying to decide between a Notrump and a Club bid. But he was afraid to bid the Notrump until he found out how the Clubs were distributed.

"Well," he drawled, his voice low and serious, "I reckon I'll bid a little Club."

Al glared challengingly.

"I'm taking you out with a Diamond!" he bawled.

Jake leaned over and whispered into Al's ear:

"One Heart, Sweetheart."

Slim hesitated and stared into Al's face as though trying to read a message there.

"I'm passing," he said.

There was silence. Jake could hear his watch ticking in his vest pocket. He felt a sense of fullness, of wellbeing; it was the first he had felt that day. He held his cards in his right hand, close together, so that he could see at a glance all the denominations he had. His eyes enveloped Bob's face with a steady, benevolent gaze.

"You got the right spirit," said Bob, turning to Slim. "I'm bidding two Notrumps!"

"Passing," said Al. "You can have it."

"Three Notrumps," Jake whispered again into Al's ear.

"Aw, nigger, cut it out!" said Al, pushing Jake back.

72

Slim looked at his hand. He had a terrible bust. But he had four Diamond cards and Al had bid Diamonds. He also had four Club cards, even though Bob had bid Clubs. Spades had not been mentioned. Slim's lips moved several times before he spoke.

"I'm ddddoubling yyou," he stammered.

"Is you crazy?" asked Bob. "Well, I'm *re*doubling."

"Pass."

"Pass."

"Pass."

"Let's go, Al," said Jake.

Al led with the five of Diamonds. Jake spread his hand. Bob pulled the seven of Diamonds from the Dummy. Slim crossed it with the ten. Bob thought fast; he blinked his eyes. He had been doubled and he had redoubled. He had better lay low this time; he was going to lose the King or the Queen anyway. He ducked the trick, playing the six of Diamonds. Jake swallowed, his stomach contracting.

"Thank you, boss," said Slim, stacking the cards.

Slim led back with the Jack of Diamonds. Bob frowned. The room became so silent that they could hear the rumble of the "L" as though it were many blocks closer than it really was. Bob was nervous and tense; he did not want to be shut out of the Diamonds. The thought that he had been doubled and that he had in turn redoubled haunted him.

"Here's the King," he sighed, laying down the King of Diamonds.

"I wouldn't touch it," said Al, playing the Deuce.

Bob pulled the four of Diamonds from the Dummy, taking the trick. He had to see what he could get out of his Hearts and see about it quickly. He took two Heart tricks with the Ace and King, but lost the Queen. Al and Slim were bossing diamonds. Slim led with the Trey, and sweat beaded on Bob's forehead. Reluctantly, he threw his poor Queen under the axe of Al's Ace. Al then turned the eight and nine of Diamonds, downing Bob's bid of three Notrumps by one. Jake and Bob sat still, gazing emptily at the backs of the cards.

"You's one down, *re*doubled!" boomed Slim, marking down the score.

"Easy's taking candy from a baby!" laughed Al.

"Smoother'n velvet!" laughed Slim, rearing back in his seat and blowing smoke to the ceiling.

"Like tolling of a log!" sang Al, shuffling the cards.

"Like sliding down a greasy pole!"

"Like snapping your fingers!"

"Like spitting!"

"Like falling in love with a high yellow!"

73

Al and Slim leaned back in their chairs and roared with laughter.

"Come on, you niggers," railed Jake. "Cut out the monkey business and play cards!"

"And don't make so Gawddamn much noise," said Bob.

"Oh, so that's it! You niggers getting just a little bit mad, hunh?" asked Al.

"They just can't take it," said Slim.

"Wait and do your gassing when the game's over," said Bob.

"And the one what laughs last is the one what laughs best," said Jake.

"Not 'less you got something to laugh about," said Al, pityingly.

"How about the way we beat you guys last Tuesday?" asked Bob.

"Oh, they forget all about such *little* things as that," said Jake.

Al and Slim rose and shook each other's hand solemnly.

"Boy, we got 'em going back to ancient history," said Al.

"We going to make 'em go back to the Garden of Eden before we gets through with 'em," said Slim.

Jake and Bob took their defeat with stoical smiles. The cards were cut, and Al dealt.

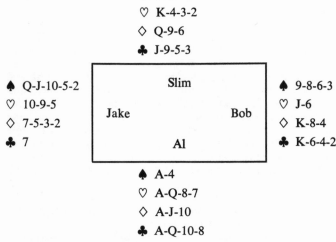

♠ K-7
♡ K-4-3-2
◇ Q-9-6
♣ J-9-5-3

♠ Q-J-10-5-2   Slim   ♠ 9-8-6-3
♡ 10-9-5   ♡ J-6
◇ 7-5-3-2   Jake   Bob   ◇ K-8-4
♣ 7   ♣ K-6-4-2
                      Al

♠ A-4
♡ A-Q-8-7
◇ A-J-10
♣ A-Q-10-8

"Let's go," said Slim.

"One Notrump," said Al.

"I ain't got a Gawddamn thing," whined Jake, squirming in his chair.

74

"Don't confess to me!" said Slim haughtily. "I ain't no priest!"

"But you can't play when you ain't got nothing," said Jake.

"What you want us to do about it?" asked Slim.

"I bet Al didn't half shuffle them cards," mumbled Bob.

"Don't get smart, nigger," said Al. "You done had your deal."

"Play cards!" Jake bawled disgustedly. "I'm passing."

"Same here," said Slim.

Bob tapped his consent. Jake led with the Queen of Spades. Slim spread his hand and Al pulled the King from it. Bob tossed in the eight of Spades, and Al put the four, taking the trick. Al paused and studied his hand and the Dummy. He wondered if he could trap the missing Diamond and Club Kings. He tried the Club, pulling the Jack from the Dummy. Bob nonchalantly tossed in the Deuce.

"Is you kidding?" asked Al, playing the eight spot from his hand. Reluctantly Jake surrendered the seven.

Al smiled and leaned toward Bob; he flexed his fingers in Bob's face as though he were a dentist about to pull a tooth.

"Just set real still and don't cry," he said. "This'll be very painless."

Slim also leaned to Jake and said:

"I hope those few lines found you well."

"Nigger, play cards!" snorted Bob.

"You guys ain't got no sense," said Jake.

Al pulled the Trey of Clubs from the Dummy; Bob still held out, giving up only the fourspot. Al crossed it with the ten. Jake discarded the Deuce of Spades.

"I'm going to murder that old King of yours," said Al, neatly stacking the trick. "Just you wait and see. Linger along, but die he must!"

Again, Al led from the Dummy, bringing out the five of Clubs. With an air of innocent unconcern Bob slid out the sixspot. Al covered it with the Queen, taking the fourth trick after Jake had sleepily discarded the Deuce of Diamonds. Al hunched his shoulders and puffed his jaws, stifling laughter.

"Come on, little baby, it ain't going to hurt none," he said, touching Bob under the chin with his finger. "Papa's doing this for your own good."

Al then banged down the Ace of Clubs with a crash that all but upset the table. Jake curled his lips and discarded the five of Spades. Al drew the ninespot from the Dummy, and turned to watch Bob. Bob turned his head and threw in the King.

"It didn't hurt much, did it, Honey?"

Al led the Queen of Hearts from his hand, taking

Jake's nine, and pulling the King from the Dummy. Bob gave up the six, giving Al his seventh trick. Mercilessly, Al finessed the Diamonds through Bob in the same way he had finessed the Clubs, trapping the King.

"Boys," announced Al, rearing back and looking blissfully at the ceiling, "I believe my soul it's a Grand Slam!"

Al turned all thirteen tricks and let out a whoop.

"Let's don't play no more," said Slim, with mock concern.

"How come?" asked Jake.

"We ain't got no competition."

"Like hell," said Bob.

"But what's the use of playing you chumps? We *know* we can beat you."

Slim rose hurriedly and grabbed his hat and coat.

"I got to send a telegram," he said.

They looked at him.

"To who?"

"For what?"

"I'm going to get in touch with old Ely Culbertson and ask 'im don't he want another partner."

Al grabbed Slim and they danced around the room. Jake sat fingering the deck with a sick smile.

"If you going to play, come on and set down," said Bob, rising. "I'll be back in a minute."

"Look what we made 'im do!" yelled Al.

"Don't drink the iodine," said Slim, coughing slightly.

Al and Slim sat again. Bob came back with his hands trembling and his eyes looking a little bloodshot. Al cut the deck and Jake began to deal.

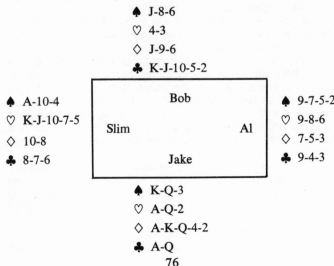

♠ J-8-6
♡ 4-3
◇ J-9-6
♣ K-J-10-5-2

Bob

♠ A-10-4
♡ K-J-10-7-5
◇ 10-8
♣ 8-7-6

Slim   Al

♠ 9-7-5-2
♡ 9-8-6
◇ 7-5-3
♣ 9-4-3

Jake

♠ K-Q-3
♡ A-Q-2
◇ A-K-Q-4-2
♣ A-Q

Jake smiled when he took up his first card, and when he had his whole hand before him a golden grin spread from ear to ear.

"What you saying?" asked Slim impatiently.

"Just a little Diamond," said Jake modestly, closing his eyes.

Bob looked at Jake, puzzled.

"Two Clubs," he said.

"Passing," said Al.

"Three Diamonds," said Jake.

"Passing."

"Four Clubs," said Bob.

Al tapped.

"Four Notrumps!" boomed Jake.

"Passing," whispered Slim.

"Five Hearts," said Bob.

"Passing," said Al. "What you guys doing? Having a contest all between yourselves?"

"Five Notrumps," said Jake.

Slim tapped.

"Six Clubs," said Bob, punching Al in the ribs.

Al threw his cards on the table and said:

"I'm passing from now on."

"Six Notrumps," said Jake.

Slim looked at his hand, and said:

"I'm doubling you on general principles!"

Bob tapped.

"Same here," said Al.

"*Re*doubled on the same general principles," said Jake.

Slim and Bob and Al tapped their consent to pass. Locked in the grip of conflicting impulses, Slim sat still and mute; then hesitantly, with his hand trembling, he led with the Jack of Hearts. Bob spread his hand. Al shook his head when he saw it. Jake pulled the Trey of Hearts from the Dummy. Al gave up the six, and Jake took the trick with the Queen. He brought back the Trey of Spades, to which Slim yielded the fourspot. Jake pulled the Jack of Spades from the Dummy. Al played the Deuce. Jake frowned, wondering who had the Ace. He counted his sure tricks; he had five Club tricks, five Diamond tricks and one Heart trick. *O, Gawd, if I can only make this a redoubled Grand Slam I'll pay 'em all back!* He grew so excited he began to sweat. Only the King of Hearts and the Ace of Spades were out against him. Somebody had held out the Ace of Spades, Al or Slim, he did not know whom. He decided to save his Heart trick till the last, hoping to catch the King. This was the best bet since the Ace of Spades was out against him. He laid down five Club tricks, taking one from his hand and four from the

Dummy. The Dummy was still in. He led the Diamond from the Dummy, turning one from the Dummy and four from his hand. Very slowly he eased the Ace of Diamonds out of his hand into Slim's face, saying:

"Come on, little baby, papa's waiting for you!"

Bob flopped deep into his chair and yelled, upsetting the table. Jake turned to him and asked with mock humbleness:

"Didn't somebody tell me a little while ago that we was playing against *champeens*?"

Bob sobered, looked thoughtful, and said:

"Seems like I did hear something like that, come to think of it. But, Holy Cats, that was too doggone easy to be against Champeens."

"You know," said Jake, putting his arms around Bob's shoulders, "I think they's gone and got mixed up as to who they *is*. *We* is the mens they *thought* they was. . . ."

Bob laughed uproariously. It was a very peculiar laugh, beginning noiselessly, a sharp expulsion of breath coming from the diaphragm; an expulsion that travelled slowly upwards, holding those who heard it in suspense, and finally cracking in a loud guffaw which terminated in something resembling a pig's squeal. Jake, galvanized by Bob's laughter, grabbed the sides of the upturned table and rolled off the chair on to the floor, his face contorted in a spasm of merriment. Each time he could regain his breath he would moan:

"Lawd . . . Lawd. . . ."

Jake and Bob laughed so long that Al and Slim began laughing. And when Jake and Bob saw that they had made their opponents laugh at their *own* defeat, they laughed harder. Presently, they stopped laughing at the joke Jake had made, and began laughing because they were all laughing. And they laughed because they had laughed. They paused for breath, and then they laughed at how they had laughed; and because they had laughed at how they had laughed, they laughed and laughed and laughed. Suddenly Slim's laugh turned into a violent cough. He stood up, bent over with his hands touching the floor, and his long thin body heaved and rocked. Jake, Al, and Bob stood about him, silent, anxious.

"Here," said Bob, offering the flask. "Drink something."

When Slim tried to swallow he coughed and whiskey splashed his vest and trousers. Finally, he forced some of it down his throat. His face was wet with sweat. They led him to the sofa; he leaned back, closed his eyes, and breathed heavily. Steam sang in the radiator and from far off came the rumble of the "L".

78

IX.

Now that Slim had stopped coughing, Jake relaxed and felt better. Slim's spells always bothered him; each time he saw Slim like that he had a feeling that he was being warned of something. He pushed himself far back in his seat, thinking, *He's all right. He's been coughing like that a long time now.* Al was sitting on the far end of the sofa, next to Slim, knotting his fingers. Jake looked around, feeling empty, missing something.

"Where Bob?"

Al grunted wearily:

"Same old place."

Jake made a pretense of laughing, but it got no further than a mere shaking of shoulders. He was relieved to see Bob coming through the door, head down, fastening his beltbuckle. It was as though someone had whispered, *It's O.K. The house ain't on fire.* He leaned back and closed his eyes. *I'm getting nervous as hell.* And he knew that as long as he sat this way his nervousness would increase. He glanced around, restless, on edge. Slim was much better; he was wiping his face with a damp handkerchief. *What to hell? Slim's all right.* Jake's mind fished about, trying to get hold of an idea to cover his feeling of uneasy emptiness. He noticed that Al was wearing a new shirt, a light green one with delicate white pencil stripes running vertically. Al's fat face rested in smug repose, and Jake wanted to disturb it, possess it, make some of the strength of that repose his own.

"So you got a new shirt, hunh, Al?" asked Jake quietly, tentatively, sucking his teeth and throwing his leg over the arm of the chair.

Al modestly stroked the collar of his shirt with his fingers.

"Yeah, I picked it up yesterday."

"Where you steal it from?"

"Steal it? Nigger, you can't steal shirts like this!"

"You didn't buy it!"

"How come I didn't? Ain't I got money?" said Al. He was sitting upright, his round black face flushed with mock indignation.

"What did you ever buy?" asked Jake.

Al rose, rammed his hands deep into his pockets, and stood in front of Jake.

"You go into Marshall Field's and *steal* a shirt! It takes kale to wear clothes like this!"

"Marshall Field's?"

"Yeah. *Marshall Field's!*"

"The closest you ever got to Marshall Field's was the showwindow," said Jake.

"That's a Gawddamn lie!" said Al.

Slim and Bob listened silently, hoping for a bout of the dozens between the two.

"Whoever heard of a nigger going into Marshall Field's and buying a *green* shirt?" asked Jake, as though to himself.

"Aw, nigger, quit signifying! Go buy *you* a shirt!"

"I don't need no shirts. I got aplenty!"

"This nigger setting here wearing this purple rag around his throat talking about he's got aplenty shirts. *Some*body wake 'im up!"

Slim and Bob laughed.

"I can change *five* shirts to your *one*," boasted Jake.

"The onliest way you can do that is to pull off the one you has on *now* and put it on *five* times," said Al.

Slim and Bob laughed again.

"Listen, nigger," said Jake. "I was wearing shirts when you was going around naked in Miss'sippi!"

Slim and Bob opened their mouths wide and slumped deep into their seats.

"Hunh, hunh," said Al. "That was the time when you was wearing your hair wrapped with white strings, wasn't it?"

"*White* strings? Aw, Jake. . . . Hehehe!" Bob could not finish, the idea tickled him so.

"Yeah," said Jake. "When I was wearing them white strings on my hair old Colonel James was sucking at your ma's tits, wasn't he?"

"Jeeesus," moaned Slim, pressing his handkerchief hard against his mouth to keep from coughing. "I told a piece of iron that once and it turned *redhot*. Now, what would a poor *meat* man do?"

Al glowered and fingered his cigarette nervously.

"Nigger," Al said slowly, so that the full force of his words would not be missed, "when old Colonel James was sucking at my ma's tits I saw your little baby brother across the street watching with slobber in his mouth. . . ."

Slim and Bob rolled on the sofa and held their stomachs. Jake stiffened, crossed his legs, and gazed out of the window.

"Yeah," he said slowly, "I remembers when my little baby brother was watching with slobber in his mouth, your old grandma was out in the privy crying 'cause she couldn't find a corncob. . . ."

Slim and Bob groaned and stomped their feet.

"Yeah," said Al, retaliating with narrowed eyes. "When my old grandma was crying for that corncob, your old aunt

Lucy was round back of the barn with old Colonel James' old man, and she was saying something like this: 'Yyyyou kknow . . . Mmmister Cccolonel . . . I jjjust ddon't llike to ssssell . . . my ssstuff. . . . I jjjust lloves to gggive . . . iit away. . . .' "

Slim and Bob embraced each other and howled.

"Yeah," said Jake. "I remembers when old aunt Lucy got through she looked around and saw your old aunt Mary there watching with her finger stuck in her puss. And old aunt Lucy said, 'Mary, go home and wash your bloomers!' "

Slim and Bob beat the floor with their fists.

Al curled his lips and shot back:

"Hunh, hunh, yeah! And when my old aunt Mary was washing out her bloomers the hot smell of them soapsuds rose up and went out over the lonesome graveyard and your old greatgreatgreat grandma turned over in her grave and said: 'Lawd, I sure thank Thee for the smell of them pork chops You's cooking up in Heaven. . . .' "

Slim grabbed Bob and they screamed.

"Yeah," drawled Jake, determined not to be outdone, "when my old greatgreatgreat grandma was smelling them pork chops, your poor old greatgreatgreat*great* grandma was a Zulu queen in Africa. She was setting at the table and she said to the waiter: 'Say waiter, be sure and fetch me some of them missionary chitterlings. . . .' "

"Mmmmm . . . miss . . . missionary chitterlings?" asked Slim, stretching flat on the floor and panting as one about to die.

"Yeah," said Al. "When my greatgreatgreatgreat grandma who was a Zulu queen got through eating them missionary chitterlings, she wanted to build a sewerditch to take away her crap, so she went out and saw your poor old greatgreatgreatgreat*great* grandma sleeping under a coconut tree with her old mouth wide open. She didn't need to build no sewerditch. . . ."

"Jeeesus!" yelled Slim, closing his eyes and holding his stomach. "I'm *dying*!"

Jake screwed up his eyes, bit his lips, and tried hard to think of a return. But, for the life of him, he could not. Al's last image was too much; it left him blank. Then they all laughed so that they felt weak in the joints of their bones.

X.

"What time you got there, Bob?" asked Jake.

"Quarter to eleven."

"We better start now. We don't want to be late."

"Yeah, we better go."

They rose, put on hats, coats, and got their canes. Just as they were about to go out of the door, Bob stepped to the mirror and straightened his tie.

"Nigger, what you looking at?" asked Al.

"Ain't that a good looking dog?" asked Bob, pointing to his reflection.

Al grabbed Bob by the shoulder and swung him around.

"It's a wonder this didn't crack that glass!"

"What you beefing about? You talk like you's a John Gilbert or something. . . ."

Al came close and whispered:

"I never will be as ugly as you is."

Jake and Slim laughed. Bob threw his arm about Al's neck and bent his head to the light.

"Look!" he called to the others. "Did you ever see anybody with kinky *eyebrows*?"

Jake and Slim clapped their hands and dropped to the floor.

"But, look!" called Al, catching Bob by the chin. "Did you ever see anybody with kinky *mustaches*?"

Jake and Slim sniffled and wiped away loose saliva with the backs of their hands.

"When a man's got kinky eyebrows he just can't *get* no uglier," said Bob.

"Gawd sure must of had the bellyache when he gave you that kinky mustache," said Al.

Bob thought quickly, wondering what he could say to answer. But Al beat him.

"Say, nigger, I bet you the hair on your chest is kinky!"

Jake and Slim grabbed their knees and moaned.

"That's a Gawddamn lie!" said Bob, hurriedly buttoning his coat.

"I'll bet you it *is* kinky," said Al, emboldened by Bob's evasiveness.

"That's a lie!" said Bob, turning away.

Al advanced and pulled off his diamond ring.

"Say, I'll bet you this against nothing that it *is* kinky!"

Jake and Slim rolled over chairs and beat their palms against their thighs.

"Come on, show us," said Al.

"Aw, nigger, go on," said Bob.

Al came close and tried to open Bob's coat.

"Come on, let's see!"

"Get away, nigger!"

"I'm going to open your shirt, so help me Gawd!" said Al, tugging.

Bob backed away.

"Listen here, nigger, if you don't get away from me I'll sock you straight in your fat puss!"

"Lawd, today!" whispered Al, prancing off triumphantly.

"Well, even if I is got kinky hair on my chest, it just goes to show I'm a man, see?"

"Yyyyyyyyeah," said Al, tiptoeing close and cooing into Bob's ear. "You's a man, but you's a uuuuuuugly man. . . ."

Jake and Slim kicked the walls of the room with the toes of their shoes.

XI.

They filed down the steps and went out. A deluge of sunshine bathed the streets and houses. The air was warm and clear. Traffic had thickened and there was a blare of auto horns. Women went in and out of stores with shopping bags filled with groceries. Boys and girls, free from school for the holiday, spun tops and played hopscotch upon the pavements in ragged sweaters. Often Jake and Al and Slim and Bob had to walk around them to keep from breaking up their game.

"Look!"

"What?"

"Where?"

"Over there. What's that going on over there?"

"Come on, let's go and see!"

A hefty, short, jet-black man was standing on the lowered rear gate of a truck haranguing passersby. He spluttered out of one corner of his mouth, his chest heaving laboriously as though he were short-winded. Each time he raised his arm for emphasis his checkered suit flapped and fluttered in the air like a flag. A red tie with a horseshoe stickpin nestled between the wings of a soiled collar, and each jerk of his neck set up a shower of white and blue sparks. His lips were plump and loose, and his little red eyes were all but drowned in the oily fat of his cheeks. A round potbelly rose and bulged over a wide belt like an inflated balloon, giving the notion that at any moment he was likely to explode, and vanish.

"Come closer, folks, come closer! Don't block the sidewalk! Step right up 'n' don't be scared!"

"Come on, let's see what he's saying."

"Yeah, move in closer."

The man placed upon a rickety card table a square box made of meshed wire. Then, before the crowd could realize

83

what was happening, he pulled out a huge rattle snake and wrapped its brown, scaly body around his neck.

"Uuuhhhh!"

The crowd marveled and fell back.

"Come closer, folks, come closer! Nothing kin bother yuh as long as Ah'm's here! Ah's got all the Powers of Evil in mah control! Come closer, folks, come closer! Ah's got a great message fer yuh."

The snake lifted its head warily and darted its blue-black tongue. In a few minutes the crowd doubled. The man smiled and stroked the snake's head with stumpy fingers. When satisfied with the size of his audience, he spoke:

"LAdees 'n' Gen'meeeeeeens: Ah'm's the SNAKE MAN! Ah wuz BO'N 'bout FORTEEEEY YEars erGO on the banks of the FAMous NILE in the great COUNtreeeeey of AF-RIker, yo' COUNtreeeeeey 'n' mah COUNtreeeey—in tha' LAN' where, in the YEars gone by, yo' FATHER 'n' mah FATHER ruled suPREME! In mah FATHER'S day the PRINCES 'n' CROWNED heads of YOURpe came t' his feets astin' fer ADVICE, astin' t' be tol' things they couldn't TELL themselves, astin' t' have things DONE they couldn't do themselves. The CROWNED heads of YOURpe respected mah FATHER—he wuz the WISE man of the NILE! Mah FRIENDS, Ah'm's mah FATHER'S son, not only in FLESH, but in SPERIT! FER TWENTEEEEEEEY YEars Ah set at mah FATHER'S feets 'n' soppedup the WISDOM OF his GREAT MIN'! T'DAY, Ah'm's here t' give YUH the beneFIT of mah FATHER'S GREAT WISDOM! Ah'm's here t' TELL yuh the SECRET of GOOD 'n' the SECRET of EVIL! Ah'm's here t' TELL yuh the SECRET of LIFE 'n' the SECRET of DEATH! . . . Be still, Patsy, be still! . . ."

He paused and stroked the rattler's scaly body.

"Say, he's from Africa!"

"Yeah, he knows a lot of secrets!"

"He sure must know something to charm that snake that way!"

"You telling me?"

". . . But 'fo' Ah goes inter that, mah FRIENDS, Ah wanna give yuh some INDIcation of mah SINGULar POW-ERS! Yuh see HERE in mah han's is TWO steel rings MADE in the FAR OFF COUNtreeeeey of JApan. Mah FRIENDS, these rings is made of SOLID STEEL, 'n' if there's anybody in this DISTINGUISHED AUDIENce, be he MALE or FEMALE, who thinks he kin BEN' or BREAK these rings he has a chance t' try 'n' win FIVE DOLLARS in COL' CASH! ANYbody wanna try? Who? *Who*? WHO? DON'T BE SCARED, FOLKS! STEP right up 'n' try!

Now, WHO wanna try? WHO? Yuh, Mister? Yes, suh! Here yuh is! TRY wid all yo' MIGHT 'n' STRENGTH! PULL HARD, Mister, PULL HARD! Why, whut's the MATTER, Mister? Can't yuh BEN' or BREAK these LITTLE rings? NAW? Sho' 'nough? Haa! Haa! Give 'em here! Waal, who else wanna try?"

"I bet I could break them Gawddamn rings!"

"I bet I could, too!"

"Let's try!"

"Say, let me at them rings, Mister!"

"Let me see if I can break 'em!"

". . . Awright, suh! Here yuh is! Yuh kin TRY! 'N' 'member, if yuh BEN' or BREAK 'em, yuh wins FIVE DOLLARS IN COL' CASH! . . . "

Jake strained with all his might against the steel rings, but could not bend nor break them.

"Whut these rings made out of?" he asked, puzzled.

"Let me try!"

"I want a hand at 'em!"

"Don't give 'em back till I get at 'em!"

They grunted, squirmed, puffed, bent double; but the little steel rings remained perfectly round, slender, shiny. Smiling sheepishly, they handed them back.

". . . Yuh couldn't BEN' or BREAK 'em, mah FRIENDS? Naw? Tha's jus' too BAD! Yuh missed FIVE DOLLARS IN COL' CASH! Waal, WHO else wanna TRY? WHO else? Who? *Who*? WHO? NOBODY? Waal, waal, mah FRIENDS, lemme show yuh something! Lemme show yuh jus' WHUT kin be done wid these rings! SEE! LOOK HARD! LOOK CLOSE! THE CLOSER YUH LOOK THE LESS YUH SEE! The han' is FASTERN'N the EYE! PRESTO! PRESTO! SEE! The rings is locked in each other. . . ."

"Jeeeesus! Yuh see that?"

"I'm looking right at 'im!"

"That guy's a wizard!"

"You telling me?"

". . . Now, mah FRIENDS, yuh wanna know jus' how Ah did it? Naw! Naw! Ah can't tell yuh tha', mah FRIENDS! Tha's not fer yuh t' know, mah FRIENDS! Tha's some of mah FATHER'S POWER, mah good, GREAT OL' FATHER who advised 'n' guided the CROWNED HEADS of YOURpe! Now, mah FRIENDS! let's git down t' bis'ness. Ah'm's here t'day t' give yuh a MESSAGE OF HOPE! Be still, Patsy, be still! Mah FRIENDS, yuh see this GLASS? Waal, it's jus' a ORD'NARY drinkin' glass, the kind yuh 'n' me drinks WATER out of! Ah'm's gonna fill this GLASS wid CLEAN PURE WATER, RAIN WATER, which is the only PURE WATER THERE IS! RAIN WATER'S the

WATER Gawd Awmighty put here for his chillun t' drink,
the WATER HE cleaned 'n' purified HISSE'F! See there! See
how clear 'tis? GAWD'S water, mah FRIENDS, GAWD'S
water! IT'S CLEAN 'N' PURE 'N' SPARKLIN', LIKE
YUH 'N' ME WUZ WHEN WE WUZ BO'N INTER THIS
DARK WORLD! Awright, so fer, so good! Now, whut happens? YUH MENS KNOWS! Yuh bergin t' treat tha' ol'
body, tha' PRECIOUS ol' body, CARELESS 'n' ROUGH,
didn't YUH? Don't la'gh, men don't la'gh! Ah'm's talkin'
t' yuh straight from the SHOULDER! This is a MATTER
of LIFE 'N' DEATH! Yuh bergin t' ketch col's, didn't
YUH? Don't la'gh, men, don't la'gh! Yuh went 'n got
married, didn't YUH? Men, Ah'm's astin' yuh *not* t' la'gh!
Cause yuh 'n' me knows a woman do take a CERTAIN
strength from a man, don't she? Mah FRIENDS, lemme
show yuh jus' whut happened t' yo' bodies durin' all these
YEars! Be still, Patsy, be still! . . ."

"Get up closer!"

"That guy's smart!"

"Yeah, he knows what he's talking about!"

". . . Yuh see this GLASS of PURE WATER? Waal,
Ah'm gonna po' jus' a little bit of this ACID inter it! Jus'
a *little* bit, see? SEE! WATCH how DARK the water
TURNS! SEE! LOOK how BLACK it's gittin'! Mah
FRIENDS, tha's whut happened t' yo' bodies! . . ."

"Geeeeeee! It turned black!"

"I wonder what was that he put in it?"

"He said it was *acid*!"

"Yeah, it must of been *acid* of some kind!"

". . . Yo' bodies is DEFILED! Ah knows jus' how yuh
FEELS when yuh gits outta bed in the MO'NIN'S! Yuh
gits up TIRED, don't yuh? There's a nasty taste in yo'
MOUTH, ain't it? Yes, mah FRIENDS, Ah knows! Them
ol' LIMBS feels like they don't wanna MOVE, don't they?
Mah FRIENDS, Ah knows! . . ."

"That guy talks like he's telling the truth."

"Yeah, I believe he knows what he's talking about, all
right."

"You know, sometimes I feels that way myself when I
gets up in the mornings."

". . . Now, mah FRIENDS, there's a CURE fer all this!
IF IT WUZN'T SO AH WOULDN'T TELL YUH! Gawd in
all HIS MIGHT 'n' GLORY'S done fixed this CURE fer
US! Does yuh think HE woulda let all this happen widout
puttin' a CURE here? Tell me, does yuh THINK tha'? O YE
OF LITTLE FAITH! Does yuh THINK HE thinks LESS
of yuh'n He do the BEES'S of the FIEL'S? Tell me, does

yuh? HIS EYE IS ON THE SPARROW 'N' AH KNOWS HE'S WATCHIN' ME! Ain't yuh got no *faith*? FAITH'S THE SUBSTANCE OF THINGS YUH HOPE FER 'N' THE EVIDENCE OF THINGS YUH CAN'T SEE! Mah FRIENDS, tha's true, 'n' 'fo' one *jot* or *tittle* of GAWD'S PRECIOUS WORD fails the HEAVEN 'n' the EARTH shall pass erway! So it wuz written, mah FRIENDS, so it wuz written! Be still Patsy, be still! . . . LIS'EN, ain't yuh never seed a little DOG noisin' erbout in the GRASS 'n' WEEDS huntin' fer SOMETHING? Sho, yuh did. Mah FRIENDS, tha' little DOG wuz lookin' fer something GAWD planted there fer HIS sake! HE WUZ LOOKIN' FER THA' HERB WHUT GAWD PUT THERE T' CURE EVER' LIVIN' THING IN THIS WORLD OF HIS'N! Mah FRIENDS, mah FATHER showed me tha' herb when Ah wuz a boy 'n' tol' me how t' fix it! AH'S GOT THA' HERB WID ME T'DAY! Looka here! Lemme show yuh a han'ful. SEE! Ain't the leaves *hard* 'n' *little*?"

"Can you see 'em?"

"Yeah, I can see 'em."

"What they look like?"

"Oh, they's just some little curlup green leaves."

". . . There ain't no herb in all the world tha' looks like THIS, mah FRIENDS! Now, lemme show yuh the power of this herb. Lemme show yuh how it *works*! SEE! Ah'm's puttin' jus' a little in this here glass of BLACK water 'n' yuh jus' stan' RIGHT where yuh is 'n' watch GAWD'S AWMIGHTY'S HAN' at work! WATCH GAWD'S HAN' MOVE 'FO' YO' EYES! LOOK! LOOK CLOSE! See how the water CLEARS! It ain't never FAILED, mah FRIENDS, it ain't *never* FAILED! THIS WATER IS NOW JUS' AS CLEAR 'N' PURE AS IT WUZ THE DAY IT COME FROM THE HAN' OF GAWD! Lis'en, mah FRIENDS, Ah'm's tellin' yuh GAWD'S truth! WHUT THESE LITTLE HERBS DID FER THIS WATER THEY KIN DO FER YUH! THEY'LL DO THIS FER YUH IF YUH'LL ONLY LET 'EM, 'N' THA'S THE GOSPEL TRUTH!"

"Hoooooooly Jeeesus! He turned that water white again!"

"Now, ain't that something!"

"He's got the real stuff!"

"That guy's a wizard!"

". . . LADeeees 'n' GEN'meeeeens, mah UNIVERSAL HERB CUREALL MEDICINE CURES NERVOUSNESS 'N' PNEUMONIA, MEASLES 'N' MENINGITIS, CORNS 'N' CANCERS, CONSUMPTION 'N' WHOOPIN' COUGH, RINGWORM 'N' RHEUMATISM, CARBUNCLES 'N'

LUMBAGO, 'N' ALL THE DIVERS AILMENTS OF THE
HUMAN BODY! It prevents as well as cures, so if yuh
ain't got nothin' t' matter wid yuh right now, git a bottle
anyhow, jus' t' make sho. . . . They's only one dollar
per bottle, LADeeees 'n' Gen'meeeeeens! Who wants one?
Awright, Mister. Jus' one dollar! Thank yuh! Awright, now,
who wants ernother one? Tha's fine! Jus' one dollar! Thank
yuh! Now, who wants ernother one? Here yuh is, lady!
Take mah word fer it! Yuh'll never be sorry yuh bought it!
Awright, jus' one dollar a bottle! Who wants ernother one?
Be still, Patsy, be still!"

"Yuh got any money?"

"Man, I ain't got penny *one*!"

"Me neither."

"I just got carfare to work."

"But I wants one of them bottles."

"Me too."

". . . Now, mah FRIENDS, if yuh ain't got a dollar
wid yuh right now, jus' step up here 'n' leave me yo' name
'n' address, 'n' Ah'll see tha' yuh gits a bottle of mah UNI-
VERSAL HERB CUREALL MEDICINE delivered right t'
yo' home BRIGHT 'n' EARLY in the mo'nin'! . . ."

After they had left their names and addresses, they walked
in the direction of the "L" station.

"You know, I'd like to study and learn something like
that," said Jake.

"Yeah, I ain't never seen nobody do the things he done."

"Me neither."

"A man must make a lot of money in a business like
that."

"He's a magician," said Jake.

"You know, that stuff might help this dose I got," said
Bob.

"And maybe it'll keep me from coughing so much," said
Slim.

"I'm going to make Lil take some of that," said Jake.
"It might save her from that operation."

"A stitch in time saves nine," said Al.

XII.

"I'm hungry."

"You ain't by yourself."

"Let's get a sandwich and a malted milk."

"I'm broke," said Jake. "Just got carfare to work and back."

"Come on. I'll stake you," said Bob.

At 47th Street and South Parkway they entered a Walgreen drugstore, took seats on stools at a white porcelain counter, pushed their hats far back on their heads, and waited to be served. Presently, a plump, mulatto girl dressed in a white and blue uniform brought four small glasses of ice water.

"What you gen'mens have?"

"What we going to eat?" asked Jake.

"Oh, I reckon I'll take one of the club sandwiches and a malted milk," said Bob, scratching his head.

"Same here," said Al. "Only make mine two sandwiches."

"Ditto," said Slim.

"Five sammies 'n' fo' malts!" the girl yelled aside out of the corner of her mouth.

"Five sammies 'n' fo' malts!" a bass voice echoed from behind a screen.

The girl swung around so that the flesh on her oversized buttocks trembled.

"Now, ain't that something!"

"The stuff's here!"

"Not bad!"

"She's at the post!"

"She's off!"

"She's a winner!"

"By five lengths!"

"Without a call!"

"That's a Packard Chassis," said Jake. "And I'll bet my bottom dollar it can run."

"You's wrong! That's a Rolls Royce Chassis, the kind I likes to drive," said Slim.

"She's built for service, all right," said Bob.

A black hand pushed from behind the screen four tall silver-looking cans and a plate of toast. The girl put the cans under electric whippers; there was a buzzing as the ice cream, chocolate, milk, and malt were mixed.

"Make it snappy, Sweetstuff!" called Jake. "We's working men and we's got a clock to punch."

"Oh, yeah?" asked the girl, bringing the malted milks.

"Yeeeeeeah," said Jake.

"Working mens is sure hard to find these days," said the girl.

"We knows it," said Bob.

"In fact, I just can't seem to find one," said the girl, lifting her eyebrows.

"You telling us?" asked Bob.

89

They laughed and the girl's face fell and her lips pouted. Seeing they would not flirt, she went to the rear of the store and turned on the radio.

. . . In the latter part of 1862 Meade and Lee sparred and feinted cautiously for an opening to deal a telling blow. . . .

"Say, that radio's talking about the Civil War!"

"This is old Lincoln's Birthday, you know."

"Yeah."

"War's a terrible thing."

"Somebody said war was hell."

"I think a guy named Herman said that."

"Yeah," said Slim. "I heard my boy talking about him the other night."

"Say," whispered Jake through a mouthful of sandwich. "That chicken ain't bad."

"Who?"

"That dame, *there*," said Jake, jerking his head.

"Aw. . . ." said Al. "A gold digger, that's all."

"Yeah," agreed Slim. "She's got 'gimme' all over her face."

"A half-white broad like that is hard as hell to manage," said Al.

"Them high yellows is stuck-up and think they's better anybody else," said Slim.

"Yeah," said Bob. "They thinks they's the whole cheese just 'cause they looks like white women."

"You guys nuts," snorted Jake. "They ain't so bad if you knows how to handle 'em."

"Oh, yeeeeeah?"

"I could make her walk a chalkline."

"You made the last yellow one you had do that, didn't you?" asked Slim.

"Oh, I didn't want that old toughmeat," said Jake.

They laughed.

"Well, how about the one you had last year?" asked Jake, scowling.

Slim took a huge bite of sandwich, ignoring him.

"Say, I'm *talking* to you!"

"Who? Me?"

"Ain't this a *bitch*!" asked Jake, laying down his sandwich and turning to the others for support.

"What *is* you talking about!" demanded Slim.

"I'm talking about that yellow gal who gutted your pocketbook last year," said Jake.

"*What* yellow gal?"

"You mean to say you don't remember when you went around here drooping like a sick chicken?"

"Hell naw!"

"You got a damn good memory, that's all I got to say!" said Jake.

They laughed; Slim sipped his malted milk as though he had not heard.

The girl came back and leaned against the counter so that the bulge in her stomach showed. She appeared to be about eighteen or nineteen, and had a clear, yellow skin. Holding her maroon-colored eyes wide and innocent, she lightly caressed her brass-tinted hair, tucking in a loose strand here and a stray curl there, pretending she was not aware of the men but only of the traffic flowing past the glass window. Her lips were full, wide, and blood-red; she wet them frequently and slowly with the tip of her tongue. She yawned, raising her elbows high above her head, exposing hairy armpits. Her fat fingers loosened and the towel she held dropped to the floor. As she bent to pick it up her dress rose and showed a naked stretch of thigh. Jake hunched Bob.

"Aw, cheap," Bob mumbled.

They finished and lit cigarettes.

"What's the damages, Gingerbread?"

"Dollar eighty?"

"Here's mine."

"And mine."

"Aww. . . ." said Bob, pushing their money back. "This one's on me. Keep the change, Sweetmeat."

"Thanks!" said the girl, exposing six gold teeth.

As they went out the radio sang:

> . . . And the whole night through Lincoln paced with his hands knotted behind his back, mumbling mournfully: Why don't they come? Why don't they come? . . .

They hurried in the direction of the "L" station.

"What's that?" asked Al.

"Sounds like music."

"Sounds like a brass band."

"A radio, maybe," said Bob as they came to a corner and paused for a red light.

"I sure wish I had dated that dame up," said Jake ruefully.

"*What* dame?"

"That dame in the drugstore."

"Jeesus! You still thinking about her?"

"She wasn't so bad," said Jake.

91

"Man, I hears a band playing somewhere."

"One of them calliopes, maybe," said Slim.

"Did you see her stommick when she leaned against that counter?" asked Jake.

"Whose stommick?"

"That mama in the drugstore."

"Aw, nuts to you!" said Bob. "Let's walk up. I got to get to a bathroom. . . ."

"Nigger, hush!" said Slim, bending over with laughter. "You'll start me to coughing."

"She wasn't so bad," said Jake again.

They crossed a street, turned a corner, and came in sight of a parade some two or three blocks away. It was led by a band whose musical instruments gleamed blindingly in sunshine.

"Gee! Let's look at this!"

"Come on!"

On a high banner made of green satin and trimmed with purple frills were words in tall letters of red:

ONWARD TO AFRICA

Young brown-skinned high school girls with dirty stockings and rundown heels stood on curbstones, clapping their hands. Scrawny waifs scurried in and out of the crowd, yelling encouragement to the musicians. Clerks in hotdog stands, drugstores, grocerystores, and drygoods stores craned their necks over counters to get a glimpse. Jake and his pals paused in the open door of a garage to watch. From their rear came the sound of a radio:

> . . . We are coming, Father Abraham, three hundred thousand more, from Mississippi's winding stream, and from New England's shore. . . .

Behind the banner came the band, playing *Onward Christian Soldiers*. Immediately in front marched a young girl twirling a long, brass baton; she was big-limbed, fleshy; she had thick red lips and deep, dark eyes. Her shoulders, draped in a black cape, were thrown back, exposing a bosom full enough to spill. She walked with short, mincing steps, her spine arched inward, her eyes half closed. She smiled a continuous smile, as though supremely satisfied. Her uniform fitted her snugly, and her body jerked in answer to every twist of the music. She twirled the gleaming brass baton so fast that it was almost invisible; she spun it in one hand and then the other; she spun it under one foot and then the other; she spun it over her head and then behind her back;

then she strutted with it resting lightly upon her shoulders as though she were carrying a precious burden. Suddenly she stopped, cut a few steps from the Charleston, Balled the Jack, crooned snatches from a popular blues song, and tripped off softly in perfect time to the music, her face severely militant, her baton held high, her buttocks trembling delicately. The men in the crowd went wild, smiting their thighs and striking one another in the back with the palms of their hands.

"Laaaaaaaawd, today!"

"Now, ain't that something!"

"The hottest stuff in town!"

"This is homecooking!"

"Strut your stuff, woman!"

"Don't give 'em nothing, gal; keep everything!"

"Look at that salty dog!"

Following the girl, an enormous grey horse pranced and struck sparks from the pavement. Sitting astride the horse's back was a fat, black man whose flesh shook like fresh jelly upon his bones. A tall, silk hat, gleaming like a newly blackened stovepipe, sat askantly upon his wooly head. His suit was sky-blue, his shoes the color of ox blood, his spats light grey with mother of pearl buttons. He wore white kid gloves and held his hands stiffly in front of him, grasping the reins self-consciously, as though he were expecting his picture to be snapped at any moment. Around his ample shoulders flapped a red, green, and black sash upon which was pinned a huge, golden, five-pointed star. The horse trampled at a side gait, and the man bowed condescendingly to the left and to the right.

"Who's that guy?" Jake asked involuntarily.

"That's the Supreme Undisputed Exalted Commander of the Allied Imperial African War Councils unto the Fourth and Last Generations," said a tall, black stranger.

"Jeeesus!" breathed Jake, his lips parting with awe.

Then came two flags: the American flag and the African flag. The African flag was composed of three wide stripes of red, green, and black. In the center was the five-pointed black star. Next came a group of men wearing black uniforms decorated with clusters of gold braid. They marched in close formation, eight abreast, their left feet hitting the pavement in unison to the beats of the music. These were the supreme generals of a mythical African republic, and the medals of unfought wars and unwon victories clinked against their uniforms with every rattle of the drums. Their shoulders were straight, their faces up, and their eyes gazed into the far distance, as though piercing concrete and steel, as though entranced by some strange mirage upon the horizon.

A yellow silk banner trimmed in blue told the public that this was the

SUPREME IMPERIAL WAR COUNCIL

Next came a group also wearing black uniforms, but with not so much gold braid. These were ordinary generals, and they marched with the glittering blades of unsheathed swords held rigidly at arm's length. Their eyes were also fastened upon the distance, but not the far distance; it was a more immediate distance, a distance in accord with their rank. A floating banner of scarlet told the public that this was the

ASSISTANT SUPREME IMPERIAL WAR COUNCIL

Next followed a group which a white banner described as the *First Motor Corps*. They were dressed simply in black uniforms, and had just a tiny sprig of gold braid on each shoulder. The gaze of their eyes did not reach beyond the bosoms and buttocks of the women on the sidewalks. Then came the Black Cross Nurses dressed in black and white uniforms, marching quickly with tight lips and proud faces. Their eyes seemed to say: "Lissen, you old white folks, we kin take care uv de wounded black soljers, but ain't none of yo' wounded white soljers gwine to git any 'tenshun here."

There were no privates in the parade.

"That's hot, ain't it?"

"You telling me?"

"Lawd, that band can *really* play!"

A black woman with three teeth missing came through the crowd passing out leaflets. Jake took one. Al, Slim, and Bob looked over his shoulders as he read.

PREAMBLE

The International Negro Uplift Association and the African Communities Council is a noble, friendly, kindly, brotherly, helpful, decent, respectable, law abiding, progressive, humanitarian, charitable, educational, instructive, constructive, institutional, benevolent, religious, fraternal, expansive, growing, and rising society; and is founded by persons desiring to the utmost to work for the general uplift of the Negro people of the world. And the members pledge themselves upon the solemn faith of their black forebears to do all in their power to conserve the rights of all Mankind, believing always in the Brotherhood of Man, Sisterhood of Woman and the Fatherhood of God. The motto of the organization is, *One God! One Aim! One Destiny!* Therefore, let Justice and Mercy be done to all Mankind, realizing that if the Strong oppresses the weak, war, floods, strife, pestilence, plague, revolution, earthquakes, cyclones, and tornadoes will forever mark the path of Man; but, with Love, Faith, and Charity towards all, the reign of Peace and Plenty will be heralded into the world, and the generations of men shall be called Blessed.

"Boy, that sounds like the Constitootion!"

"They sure got a lot of brains to write something like that!"

"Yeah, they's smart."

"Come on, man! We going to be late."

"You know what I don't like about them folks?" asked Jake.

"What?"

"They wants us to go back to Africa."

"I don't like that, neither."

"They's sure nuts on that point."

"And if we went back to Africa, what would we do?"

"You'll have to ask them that."

"Aw. . . . They nuts as hell," said Jake, with an impatient wave of the hand.

They passed a beauty parlor and the scent of burning hair stung their nostrils. From a doorway a black woman stepped to the sidewalk and came briskly forward. Her hair was shining jet, and was brushed straight back, plastered to her head. The contrast between the overdose of white powder and the natural color of her skin was so sharp that she looked like two people instead of one; it was as if her ghost were walking in front of her.

"She's ready!"

"She's mellow!"

"She's pig meat!"

"Naw, she's gnat's liver!"

"Laaaaawd, today!"

Turning quickly into the "L" station, they mounted steel steps, laid their dimes upon the till, went through the revolving gate, and stood upon the platform, waiting for the train. They could still hear the dying strains of the band even above the roar of the traffic. They did not talk; they were feeling the surges of memory the music had roused in their minds. They did not agree with the parade, but they did agree with the music. There came upon them the memories of those Sunday mornings in the South when they had attended Church.

"You know," said Jake, out of the depths of a confused mood, "maybe them folks is right, who knows?"

"Maybe so."

"Wait a minute," said Bob. "I'll be right back!"

"You can't!" said Slim. "Here comes the train now."

Bob stood still and looked hard at the dirty planks of the platform.

"This thing is killing me," he mumbled.

They laughed and Slim started coughing. The train roared up and they took seats facing one another. Bob sat tense, his knees close together. Slim heaved into his handkerchief. Al fished in his pockets for a match to pick his teeth, and failing to find one, closed his eyes, leaned back, and sighed. Jake bent forward and looked at his dim reflection in the windowpane. When Slim's coughing subsided, he sat hunched and drummed his fingers nervously on the windowsill. Bob crossed his legs with a slow, tender motion and pulled his hat far down over his eyes.

"This 'L' is sure running slow," he sighed.

"Take it easy," said Jake.

"It won't kill you," said Al.

The "L" clacked rhythmically over steel rails and the buildings flying past grew taller. They blinked their eyes each time sunlight flickered in and out of the coach. Obliquely across the aisle a white woman propped her feet upon a vacant seat, exposing the curved ascent of white thighs. Jake nudged Bob with his elbow.

"Look," he whispered.

"Hunh?"

"Look!"

"What?"

"Jeeesus, you blind!"

Bob looked.

"Laaaaawd," he breathed.

Stealthily, Bob kicked Slim.

"Slim!"

"Yeah?"

"Look, *fool*!"

Slim looked and his mouth dropped open. He hunched Al.

"Al, look at the woman!"

"Where?"

"Over there, nigger!"

Al looked.

"Wheeeeeeeeeeeee!" he whistled softly.

They moved in their seats as though on pins, looking alternately at the woman and out the window. Finally, Jake rolled his eyes heavenward and sang in an undertone:

96

"Oh, Lawd, can I ever, can I ever? . . ."

Bob screwed up his eyes, shook his head, and answered ruefully:

"Naw, nigger, you can never, you can never. . . ."

Slim sat bolt upright, smiled, and countered hopefully:

"But wherever there's life there's hope. . . ."

Al dropped his head, frowned, and finished mournfully:

"And wherever there's trees there's rope."

Jake grabbed his sides, threw back his head, and let out a long laugh. Slim tried to laugh, but began heaving into his handkerchief. Bob sat with a mixed expression of pain and ecstasy. Al gripped his knees and howled. They kept so much noise that passengers turned and stared, wondering what on earth was the matter with those four black men.

Part Two:

SQUIRREL CAGE

. . . Now, when you study these long, rigid rows of desiccated men and women, you feel that you are in the presence of some form of life that has hardened but not grown, and over which the world has passed . . . .

—Waldo Frank's *Our America*

. . . It was the most difficult period of Lincoln's life. General Lee launched a furious and bitter offensive against the Union lines, inflicting murderous damage; during seven gory days thirty-six thousand men gave up their lives. Then Buell and Bragg locked horns in a desperate scramble on Tennessee soil in which eight thousand men were slain. With some fifty thousand men U. S. Grant clutched at Vicksburg and failed, leaving thousands dead upon the field. The Rebel's deadly and insistent hammerblows at the Union lines had set the War Department in Washington in a panic. . . .

I.

When the train stopped at the Congress Street "L" Station, they hurried off the platform, through the swinging gates, down the narrow stairs, and swung westward along Jackson Boulevard. Noon crowds jammed the sidewalks. It was getting cold; from Lake Michigan a stiff wind blew, rustling the flags draped over doorways. The Loop sky was murky with smoke and the sun hung like a dim red ball above the tops of skyscrapers. With the hard heels of their shoes clicking on the pavement, the four men walked silently and looked in the show windows at the new spring styles.

The clang of traffic, the array of color, and the riot of flickering lights infected Jake with a nervous and rebellious eagerness. He did not want to leave all this life in the streets; he had a feeling that he was missing something, but what it was he did not know. His teeth seemed gritty and he held them on edge in a tight clamp. He moved with a sort of slinking, swaying motion, something like a sick cat, with the handle of his cane hooked over his forearm and his hands thrust deep into his coat pockets. When he became aware of his tense anxiety, he knew he had been worrying about Lil. Had she been here already? Was this the show-down? Would Doc Higgins do as he had promised? Would he be called up before the Board of Review today? *If Doc can't fix things and Lil's done been here I'm in one helluva mess!* Yes, if Doc could not help him he would have to get busy and prepare a good lie to tell the Board of Review. He tried to remember what lies he had told in the past, but could not. He would have to prepare something new and strong this time. And looming ahead of him were eight long black hours of work. He was already tired and a little sleepy.

They paused for the red light at State Street, and when the green flashed, hurried across, down to Dearborn Street, then to the employees' entrance of the Chicago Post Office. It was a huge, dark grey building, almost the color of the sky, occupying a square block. Just to look at it depressed Jake. A sudden sense of all the weary hours he had spent within those blackened walls filled him with foreboding. As he mounted the steps he wondered if he would have to go on this way year after year 'til he died. Was this *all*? Deep in him was a dumb yearning for something else; somewhere or other was something or other for him. But where? How? All he could see right now was an endless stretch of black postal days; and all he could feel was the agony of standing on his feet till they ached and sweated, of breathing dust till he spat black, of jerking his body when a voice yelled.

"Lawd, I'd give my right ball to be off today," he sighed.

"It ain't you, it's me," said Bob.

"Every day in this joint's a nail in my coffin," said Slim.

"When you planning on going west for that cough of yours?"

"They won't give me a transfer."

"But what you going to do?"

"What to hell can I do?"

"Look like it's getting colder," said Jake as they fell into the line that was forming in the doorway.

"Yeah," sighed Al.

They got their badges and held them in the palms of their hands as the line inched forward. Jake looked at the skinny red neck of a white man and felt somebody breathing hot on the back of his own neck. He swallowed and blinked his eyes, hating all this. He fingered the silver coins in his pocket and their soft clink made him remember that he was almost broke.

"Say, youall?" he called. "Will you sign for me today? I got to get a loan from old Jones."

"I can't sign," said Al. "I owe two hundred in there already."

"How about you, Bob?"

"I'll sign."

"And you, Slim?"

"Yeah, I'll sign."

"That means we'll have a blowout tonight," said Jake gleefully. "It's on me!"

"Swell!"

They finally passed the armed guard who was inspecting the badges and monotonously saying: "O. K." A wave of dust struck their eyes and nostrils as they waded through an ocean of gloom and letter racks. A penetrating drone hovered persistently, filling their bodies with a faint, nervous tremor. Here and there, like dull, glowering eyes, were dingy lights partly hidden by green shades. The clatter of cancelling machines rose like the rumble of an underground volcano. Turning to the left, they went down a short flight of stairs and into the Post Office swingroom. It was a large, barn-like place crowded with small tables. Bob hurried off to the right, in the direction of the mens' washroom. Al, Slim, and Jake pushed their way to the checking counter where they got numbered slips of paper in exchange for their hats, coats, and canes. From the stairway white clerks and black clerks with spent, washed-out faces were coming off duty, pouring into the canteen, shouting, laughing. Jake wished that his eight hours were already put in; he wished that he were among those about to go home, to shows, to taverns, or to some lively flat where a party would be held. He stood with a wry smile on his face and answered greetings.

"What you saying, Jake?"

"Ain't saying."

"How goes it, Jake?"

"Slow, Jim. How's the mail up there?"

"She's light right now, but they's expecting it to be heavy's a dog."

He heard the clerks shouting at one another.

"Aw, Sid, don't go home! Let's play some bridge!"

"O.K. Get you a partner!"

"Say, Horace, you going home?"

"Let's eat first!"

"Lawd, am I tired?"

The white clerks got their hats and coats and hurried up the stairs. Many of them carried books under their arms; most of them were young students who regarded their jobs in the Post Office as something temporary to tide them through the University. Jake scowled as he watched their tense, eager faces. *Them white boys always in a hurry to get somewhere. And soon's they get out of school they's going to be big shots. But a nigger just stays a nigger.* He turned and looked toward the tables; many of the Negro clerks had remained to play bridge.

"White folks sure is funny," Jake said to Slim.

"How's that?"

"They don't never set down and take things easy."

"Hell, naw," said Al. "They figgering on how to get up in the world."

"They rush about like bees."

"Yeah, but ain't no use of a black man rushing."

"Naw, 'cause we ain't going nowhere."

"When a black man gets a job in the Post Office he's done reached the top."

"We just as well take it easy and have some fun, 'cause the white folks got us hog-tied."

Tables began to rattle from the thud of cards being whacked down. Hoarse shouts cut through the smoky air. Though there were no written rules of segregation, it was generally assumed that Negroes would occupy one end of the canteen and whites the other. However, if a mixture was found nothing was said. But Jake always felt that he wanted to sit with his own race because he did not know the whites so well. He definitely preferred the company of

103

his own color; they understood him and he understood them.

"You reckon old Jones is in his office?" Jake asked.

"Hard to tell. This is a holiday, you know."

"Gee, I almost forgot that! What time you got?"

"It's fifteen after twelve."

"Come on. We got time to pull the deal," said Jake.

"Let's wait for Bob."

When Bob came they raced up the stairs, and a minute later stood in a stuffy office facing a fish-eyed white man who sat behind a battered desk.

"Hello, Jake!"

"How you, Mister Jones?"

"Fair. Howdy, boys!"

Bob, Al, and Slim murmured greetings and crowded close.

"Well, what's on your mind?"

Jake hesitated, hung his head, smiled, scratched his chin, his lip, and drawled:

"I'm broke."

"You're always broke, Jake."

"But I'm in trouble this time."

"What seems to be the matter?"

"Well, you see, my wife's got to be operated on."

"That's too bad. And you're looking for dough, eh?"

"That's the truth! My wife's going to the hospital and I got to have a hundred dollars."

"How can you pay back a hundred dollars?" asked Jones, tilting in his swivel chair.

Jake blinked.

"I'm working every day. I'll pay you back like I been paying all the time."

"Yes, but. . . ."

"I done borrowed money from you before and paid it back, ain't I?"

"Yes, you have, but. . . ."

"But *what?*"

"Well," said Jones, sighing and toying with a black inkwell on his desk. "I'd advise you to have a talk with Swanson or somebody on the Board of Review. I've word from upstairs not to issue any loans to clerks whose jobs are uncertain."

"Un . . . Un*cer*tain? How? Mister Jones, I still got my job. How come you say that?"

"You'd better see the Board," said Jones, setting the ink-well down firmly. "If you come out all right with them, then come back and see me."

Jake stood before the desk, head down, the tips of his fingers resting nervously on a green blotter. He was conscious of a vague numbness creeping down his shoulders. Was this Lil's trick? *Is she done been here already?*

104

"Is she done been here already, Mister Jones? My wife?"

"You'd better see the Board, Jake," said Jones, thumbing through a pile of papers.

When outside the door Jake spat and growled:

"Gawddamn her guts! She's done it!"

"But didn't Doc say he was going to fix it?"

"She beat us to it."

"You better go and see that Board and talk like hell," said Al.

"Look here, Bob," said Jake. "I want you to do something. What time you got?"

"It's eighteen after twelve. We check in at twelve-thirty."

"Listen! While I'm at the Board, go down and 'phone Doc for me, see?"

"Sure!"

"Tell 'im I'm in for it! Tell 'im Lil's done been here and done her dirty work! Ask 'im can't he do *some*thing! Ask 'im to 'phone old Swanson right *now*."

"O.K.," said Bob, running for the stairs.

"What you going to tell the Board?" asked Slim.

Jake did not answer; he dragged his left foot slowly across the steel and spat again:

"Gawddamn that bitch's soul!"

"Anything I can do, Jake?" asked Al.

"You know I'm with you," said Slim.

"Aw, it's all right," Jake drawled, squinting out over rows and rows of letter racks. "You guys go on. I'll see you later."

They left him standing in the middle of the steel floor, just opposite the stairway. He wanted to give Bob time to get in touch with Doc Higgins before he went upstairs; he walked slowly over to a wall and leaned against it. That sense of uneasiness which had haunted him all day descended now with abrupt finality, and became real. This was it. He could not dodge any longer. The best thing to do was to go up and face that Board and have done with it. *They can't kill me,* he thought desperately. *All they can do is just fire me.* But he knew that he did not want them to do even that; he knew that by taking such an attitude he was trying to fool himself, trying to muster up false courage. But in order to *keep them* from firing him, what could he tell? He moved toward the foot of the stairs, seeing Lil's face hovering before him. Involuntarily the muscles of his arms flexed with a desire to reach out and clutch her throat. He would settle with her. Just wait until he was off from work, just wait until tonight. *What I'm going to do to her won't be funny!*

It was hard climbing the stairs with clerks jostling him

and shouting at one another, over and around him. Their indifference seemed somehow an insult; he wanted to tell these clerks about this terrible thing Lil had done, he wanted them to know what a pickle of a fix she had gotten him into. *It's all my own fault,* he thought regretfully. *I should've tricked her before she tricked me.* . . . . When he reached the third floor he remembered Bob's threat to throw up everything, to quit his job to get even with his wife. Yes, he ought to do that. He ought to walk out of here right now and never be seen or heard of again. Then Lil would be stranded and sorry. *She'd see what a fool she's been.* But if he did that, what was he to do afterwards? Where could he find work? He was broke and there were a thousand men, black and white, waiting to take his job. *If I had only saved some money during these long years I would drop Lil and this lousy job flat. I'd leave this place before you could spit!* He walked around a narrow, circular balcony and stopped before a door, trembling. *Doc sure ought to could do something.* His impulses were deadlocked and his under-wear stuck to his skin with hot sweat. He swallowed three times before he could bring his hand to touch the doorknob. *Aw, hell,* he thought again, screwing up his courage as he pushed the door in, *they sure can't kill me.* A white ste-nographer paused with her fingers suspended over the keys of her typewriter, and asked:

"Whom do you want to see?"

"Mister Swanson, Ma'm."

"The name?"

"Jackson, Jake Jackson."

"Just a moment."

She pushed a button and spoke softly into a transmitter. Presently a white man appeared in the rear door of the office.

"Oh, hello, Jake!"

"How you, Mister Swanson?"

"You want to see me?"

"Yes, sir. I want to see the Board."

"Oh, yeah!" said Swanson, nodding. "We were just about to send for you. Come on in."

Jake walked into a small office and took a seat on the edge of a chair. The office contained three desks, at two of which sat white men, and at the third a Negro. *There's that Gawddamn nigger Howard,* Jake thought bitterly. *He would have to be here.* Howard sat with a green fountain pen poised in his long black fingers.

"So you're in to see us again, hunh, Jackson?" asked Howard.

"Yeah, but what for?" asked Jake, shifting his feet around.

"Don't *you* know?" Howard asked.

"Naw."

"Well, what did you come in here for?" asked Swanson. "We weren't going to send for you for another hour yet."

"Oh, yes, sir! I . . . I was trying to get a loan from Mister Jones. He told me to come in here."

"What do you want with a loan?"

"Well, my wife's sick."

"And Jones wouldn't let you have it?"

"Naw, sir. He said to come and talk with the Board."

"You make $2,100 a year, don't you, Jake?"

"Yes, sir."

"What do you do with your money?"

"Why, I spends it to live."

There was a short silence.

"We want to have a serious talk with you, Jackson," said Howard.

The two white men wagged their heads and smiled. Howard beat a soft tattoo on the desk with his fountain pen. Jake sat awkwardly, looking from one to the other, trying to feign innocent bewilderment. *Yeah, it takes a black sonofabitch to rub it into his own people!*

"Draw your chair up closer, Jake," Swanson said.

"Yes, sir."

Jake looked again at Howard and wished that that Negro was anywhere right now but here. *How can I talk to these white folks with that nigger setting watching me? If I try to beg 'em to go easy on me, he'll think I'm a Uncle Tom. . . .* A sense of shame spread over him. *He's setting there at that desk just like he's a white man. Hell, he's the one who's a Uncle Tom!* He saw Swanson light a cigar and lean back in his chair. The room was quiet save for the faint hiss of steam in the radiator and the soft clacking of the stenographer's typewriter in the outer office. An itchy feeling, like a tiny trickle of hot water, oozed down the center of his back. He knew he should have been talking, but he did not know what to say. He did not know how much Lil had told. He carried his hand nervously across his forehead and licked his lips.

"Jake, do you know of any reason why you should be in the Postal Service?" asked Swanson.

He flinched in spite of himself; he had been expecting something, but nothing this cold, this final.

"Yes, ssssir. . . . I do my work, don't I?"

"We're asking *you*," said Swanson.

"I want to make a living for my family," Jake spluttered.

"So do a million other men," said Swanson.

107

He knew he had been put on the defensive, and he decided desperately to turn the tables.

"How come you talk to me like this, Mister Swanson? There ain't been no complaint against me, is there?"

The tip of Swanson's cigar glowed red; he took it out of his mouth and turned to the other white man, an elderly, grey-haired one.

"You want to tell him, Anderson?"

Anderson in turn looked at Howard.

"You want to tell 'im, Howard?"

Howard looked at Jake and laughed.

"Well, look like it's my dirty work," he said, laying the fountain pen aside. "Listen, Jackson, have you been doing anything that would make you unfit for the Postal Service?"

"Naw! What you mean?"

"Your wife was in this morning."

"You mean she come *here*?"

"She did."

"How come she do that?"

"You can't guess?"

"I swear to Gawd I can't!"

"She lodged a complaint against you."

"Lawd, have mercy!" Jake exclaimed. "I know what you guys talking about now! Shucks, that ain't *nothing*! Youall got me dead wrong. . . ." He paused, ignoring Howard, and turned to Swanson. "Mister Swanson, she don't know what she's doing! She's sick and nervous! She's been acting queer like that for a long time now. She's got to be operated on. I was just in to see Mister Jones in the Credit Union, trying to get some money to have her sent to the hospital. . . ."

"What do you mean? Your wife's acting queer?"

"She just don't know what she's doing!"

"Why don't you have her observed?" asked Anderson.

"What's that?"

"Why don't you have her watched to see what's wrong with her?"

"Shucks, I see her every day. I know what's wrong with her."

"I mean, if she's that bad, why don't you send her to the psychopathic?"

"To Mister who?"

"To the crazyhouse," said Howard, twisting down the corners of his mouth.

"I never thought of that," said Jake, blinking.

"Jake, this is the third time you've been before us in the last six months," said Swanson.

"I just couldn't help them other times, Mister Swanson."

"You were before us for drinking on the job once."

"But I ain't never been drunk on the job no more."

"And then you were in for debt dodging."

"It was my wife! She makes them debts! She. . . ."

"We're not interested in who makes them," said Howard. "They're yours. You should handle your affairs so they won't come into this office. This isn't a nursery."

"Yes, sir. I knows that. . . . Now, if you just let me handle my wife this time. . . ."

"Haven't you *already* handled her?" asked Anderson.

"How you mean?"

"Your wife says you beat her."

"Naw, sir! That's a lie and Gawd knows it!" Jake ran to the desk, the muscles of his face jerking. "I swear before Almighty Gawd I ain't never touched that woman! She's just out of her head! I wouldn't hit a sick woman. . . ." He became strangled, coughed, swallowed. "Mister Swanson, I'll tell you what's wrong, I'll tell you the *whole* story! That woman ain't got cat sense! She keeps me head over heels in debt. She treats me like I'm a buzzard! She wants a fur coat and a piano and I can't get 'em for her. You gentlemens knows how much money I make, and how on earth can I buy things like that for her? She threatened me and said she was coming down here and say I beat her if I didn't buy 'em. Now she's done done it. . . ." He looked at the floor, overcome with the villainy of it. "How could she live if I wasn't taking care of her? Mister Swanson, youall can't hold me responsible for a crackbrained woman! She told youall them lies for pure evil black spite. . . ."

"Her arms were black and blue with bruises," said Anderson.

"I slept with her last night and I ain't seen no bruises," said Jake.

"Where did she get 'em from?" asked Howard.

"She must have done it herself, 'cause Gawd Almighty knows I didn't do it."

"How on earth could she do that?"

"I don't know. All I know is, *I* didn't do it!"

"She says you kicked her in her side with your foot."

"Kicked her!" Jake stepped back with amazement. "Kicked her? Do I look like a man what would kick a *sick* woman?"

"We're not concerned with how you look," said Swanson.

"Mister Swanson, please, you got to listen to me! As Gawd in Heaven's my judge, I done done all I can for that woman. I done done as much as any man *could* do! For seven years that woman's been sick on my hands, and for seven years I done paid them doctor bills. I owe five hundred dollars

109

right now. . . . I ain't the kind of a man what would kick a sick woman! Youall knows I wouldn't do nothing like that. . . ."

"I'm sorry, Jake," sighed Swanson. "It's reached the point where we can't believe you any longer."

Jake glanced at Howard, swallowed his shame, and plunged desperately.

"Mister Swanson, I'm a black man. You can see my skin. I loves my race. I'm proud to be black. I wouldn't do nothing on earth to drag my race down. I ain't the kind of a man what would beat his wife and stand here before you white gentlemens. . . ."

"How long was your wife acting queer?"

"Well, for about three months, anyway."

"What did she do to make you think she was acting queer?"

"She did everything. She throwed my money away. She ran around with other men. That's how come she's sick now, running with other men. That's how come she got a tumor. . . . Mister Swanson, listen, I bet I know how come she got them bruises! She got 'em from that guy she's fooling with! He beat her. . . . He. . . ."

"That's enough, Jake," said Swanson, swinging around and pulling out a drawer. "Here's a form for your resignation. Fill it out and have it back to us by the fifteenth of the month. Your pay ends on this period."

"Mister Swanson, for Gawd's sake!"

"That'll be all!"

Jake stood stonily, his right hand raised, his mouth open. "Youall just *can't* throw a man off his job like this!"

"You're throwing yourself off, Jackson," said Howard.

"You can give me just one more chance, Mister Swanson."

"You've had three chances."

"Youall don't know what I done been through with. . . ."

"We're not concerned with that."

Jake's eyes burned and the room blurred; when he spoke his voice quavered.

"I done worked hard all these long years for the government. I ain't bothered nobody. I'm just a poor, hardworking black man. I ain't got nothing and Gawd knows I ain't never going to have nothing. I was a good worker. Youall knows I was. My life ain't been no bed of ease. I done had it hard all my days and I ain't complained. Now youall can have just a little mercy on me. Just a *little*. . . . Please, youall, give me one more chance. . . . Just *one* more. . . ."

"You're not doing yourself any good by carrying on that way," said Howard, shaking his head.

The telephone rang. *Lawd, I hope that's Doc!* Swanson

lifted the receiver. Jake eased back to his seat and wiped sweat from his face.

"Hello!"

". . . ."

"Yeah, this is he."

". . . ."

"Who? Doc Higgins? Yeeeah. . . ."

". . . ."

"Well, I don't know. It's pretty bad."

". . . ."

"This is the third time in six months."

". . . ."

"No."

". . . ."

"Did the Post Master say that?"

". . . ."

Swanson sighed and looked at Jake.

"How much? Oh, all right. . . ."

". . . ."

"Now listen to me: If I do, it's the very last time, you hear?"

Jake knew it was Doc. *If he can only get me out of this*! He looked at Howard. *Gawddamn nigger licking white folks' boots*! The receiver clicked. Swanson faced Jake.

"How long have you been working here, Jake?"

"Gong on nine years, now."

"Why can't you do better than you're doing?"

"I'll do better, Mister Swanson."

"I don't want you to come into this office no more than you want to come in here."

"Yes, sir. I know."

"Hereafter, you keep your business *out* of here!"

"Yes, sir. My wife ain't *never* coming in here no more!"

"This is the last time you're coming before us, you hear? Next time you won't even be given a hearing. We're getting tired of this!"

"Yyyyyou mmmmean I get another chance?"

"Yes, but you don't deserve it. . . ."

"Thank you, sir! Thank you!"

"All right! Get to work!"

As he went through the door Howard's pitying smile caught his eye and lingered in his mind, rankling, bitter. When he was at the bottom of the steps he stopped and stared, stared through the brick and steel walls of the Post Office, stared all the way to the South Side of the city where Lil was. *I'm going to break that bitch's neck if it's the last thing I ever do! I'm going to stomp her guts out as sure as my name's Jake Jackson. . . .*

111

II.

"How you come out, Jake?"

Bob tugged at his sleeve.

"Wasn't nothing to it," Jake answered, grinning. "How can they work the United States mails without *me*?"

"Doc fix it?"

"Sure! He 'phoned in when I was getting my walking papers."

"You sure one lucky dog. I thought you was a goner."

"And was I sweating? But wait till I get my hands on that bitch!"

"Say, I wouldn't bother her for awhile. . . ."

"The only reason I don't is 'cause I can't find her."

"Oh, yeah. Doc told me to tell you it'd cost you a hundred and fifty."

"Hundred and fifty? My Gawd! Aw, well. . . . I guess it was worth it. If he hadn't've done something I would've had no job."

"Come on! There's Al and Slim!"

They hurried to the Mailing Division.

"What happened?"

"You beat the rap?"

"Smooth as butter," said Jake, waving his palm with nervous bravado, still hot and wet with sweat. "They can't keep a good man down."

They got their timecards from the racks and punched in. A voice was bawling:

"LINE UP FOR DETAIL!"

As they fell into line and moved toward the Detail Station, they could hear the detail clerk barking out numbers.

"Jake Jackson," called Jake when he was opposite the desk.

"Ten on table nine!"

"Robert Madison," called Bob.

"Eleven on table nine!"

"Albert Johnson," called Al.

"Twelve on table nine!"

"Nathan Williams," called Slim.

"Thirteen on table nine!"

With heads bent, they shuffled across the steel floor in the direction of the tables.

A post office table is a heavy, oblong, wooden contrivance resembling generally a dining room table, only much larger and sturdier. It is supported by six to eight wooden posts and stands about three feet from the floor, coming in height up to the average man's belt. It's surface, usually about eighty feet square, is formed into a shallow trough by a five-inch bordering of wood; its bottom is covered with a thin sheeting of smooth steel. Upon these tables sacks of mail are dumped indiscriminately as they come in from the mail trucks. It is the duty of clerks assigned here to sort this mail according to size, weight, and class. Long business letters are called "lumber", and are sorted, faced leftward with the stamp turned downward into small wooden or steel trays. Ordinary correspondence letters are called "small", and are stacked likewise, but to one end of the trays and to themselves. When these trays are filled they are carried to the cancelling machines where the letters are postmarked. Special delivery and airmail letters are put to one side in a corner of the table to be collected by a clerk whose sole duty is to see that they are dispatched immediately to their proper sections for speedy service. All second, third, and fourth class mail is thrown into labeled gurneys. For eight long hours a clerk's hands must be moving ceaselessly, to and fro, stacking the mail. At intervals a foreman makes rounds of inspection to see that all is going well. Under him works a legion of cat-footed spies and stoolpigeons who snoop eternally. Along the walls are slits through which detectives peep and peer.

Jake, Al, Bob, and Slim stood at table nine rolling their sleeves and adjusting their trays.

"Another day another dollar."

"A million days a million dollars."

"Reckon we'll ever make it?" asked Al.

"Don't know, boy, don't know," said Slim, shaking his head.

"We'll have to save more'n a dollar a day to make a million," said Bob.

"And we'll have to live a thousand years," said Jake.

"It's a bitch," said Al.

"It's more'n a bitch," said Slim with a deep sigh.

"The work ain't hard and the boss ain't mean," sang Al.

"Just like lard from New Orleans," sang Bob.

They laughed.

"That song's a lie," said Jake.

"You telling me?"

"Old Uncle Sam's sure mean to his black boys," said Al.

"He's got us under his thumb and we can't rise no higher'n he wants us to," said Slim.

"You ever hear of a uncle treating his nephews like Uncle Sam treats us?" asked Bob.

"Hell, naw!"

"It ain't in the books!"

"It's 'cause we's *black* nephews."

113

"You know how come he treats us this way?" asked Jake.
"How come?"
"Uncle Sam's sister was raped by a nigger. . . ."
They laughed again.
"Jake, you crazy!"
"Well, she must've been raped," said Jake. "I can't figger out no other reason why the white folks hate us so."

He lifted a full sack of mail from a truck, tossed it to the table, dragged it toward him, dumped it, and flung the empty bag over his shoulder into a canvas gurney. He rubbed his hands together and looked at the mail. He did not want to touch it. Then he began to sort, letter by letter. The cold mail chilled his fingers. Already his throat was getting dry from dust; he wished he had remembered to buy a plug of tobacco. He heard Slim's cough bubbling in his throat incessantly, like water bubbling in a fountain. Bob stood about a foot away from the table, half bent over, afraid to let the bordering of wood touch his middle anywhere. In order to take as much weight off his feet as possible, Jake leaned heavily against the table as he worked. His feet began to sweat and the calves of his legs numbed slowly. As time passed all the noises gradually fused into one general din and imperceptibly dulled his senses. A strong light directly above his head worried his eyes and he looked at it about every five minutes, frowning. The eight long hours loomed ahead like a series of black pits, and he tried not to think of them. He could not find a suitable position for his body; he rested his weight on one side for a few moments and then the other. He crossed his feet, uncrossed them, stood awhile with one foot on top of the other, then straightened, sighing. The edge of an envelope caught irritatingly under the tip of a thumbnail and he threw it aside with such violence that Slim asked with concern:
"What's the matter?"
"Nothing," he breathed.

When his first tray was filled he carried it to a scale.
"What's the weight?" a clerk called.
"Nineteen pounds," Jake answered.
"O.K."

The weight of his tray was jotted into a huge black ledger. He piled the mail on a long counter in front of a row of cancelling machines and came back to the table. He looked at Al, whose black face rested in an expression of calm vacuity. Al's fat hands moved one over the other, stacking the mail. He was talking to a white clerk who stood at his side; his voice droned, heavy, musical, satisfied. Jake wished he had been near Al so he could have talked with him; there was something in Al which always made him feel

114

sure of himself. And Al was a soldier, a member of the Illinois National Guard. For over a year now Al had been worrying him to join. *Maybe it wouldn't be a bad idea to get into that thing.* Al was a swell fellow, easy to get along with. *It'd be hot if I could get into his company. . . .*

As the first two hours dragged by he began to feel a vast emptiness, a sort of black, resigned peace; he felt like a man who had clung to the vertical surface of a wall so long by his fingernails, hanging by his own weight, that he had grown used to it. Conscious thought drifted away and he became aware of the dark part of his blood and nerves, whispering, suggesting, counselling. His body waxed warm and the images of his mind swirled into a huge grey blot. He grew pleasurably conscious of where the table pressed against his loins, and he leaned against it harder. His genitals began to swell; his eyes did not move from the mail; his lips became moist and hung loose; he was a little dizzy; he straightened suddenly, uttering a curse to himself with a soft expulsion of breath, *Gawddamn. . . .*

"Say, Jake?"

"Hunh?"

"I was talking to old Slaughter of the N.A.A.C.P. this morning. He told me them guys in Washington's planning to send a commission down here to investigage how we colored clerks work."

"To investigate *us?*"

"That's what he said."

"How come they want to do that?"

"Well, somebody in Congress done said we ain't working like the white clerks."

"That's a Gawddamn lie!"

"They just doing that 'cause there's more black clerks working in the Mailing Division than whites."

"Slaughter was saying that the white clerks around here's done got up some kind of organization to run us and the Jews out."

"Well, the white folks didn't want this job when times was good."

"No white man wanted to work nights and breathe all this dust."

"And now 'cause the Depression's on, they want to kick us out."

"Look like the white folks don't want us to have *nothing!*"

"Ain't there some kind of union running on this job?"

"Yeah, but it ain't no damn good."

"Unions ain't nothing but a gyp game."

"And most unions don't want no black members nohow."

"This is the way I feel about it. I don't want to belong

to nothing the white folks don't want me to belong to. I ain't going to lick their boots."

"If white folks could make us buy the air we breathe, they would."

"They always cooking up something to make trouble."

"Wonder how they think we's going to live?"

"They ain't thinking about that."

"This is about the best job a black man can get and they don't even want us here."

"It's sure hell when you think about it."

"And thinking don't help none."

"Naw, you'll go nuts then."

"I wonder what'll ever happen to black folks!"

"Gawd only knows."

"The white man's Gawd in this land."

"If he says you live, you live."

"And if he says you die, you die."

"Let's check out to the can," called Bob.

Al laughed.

"Is it breaking you down, Bob?"

"Honest to Gawd, sometimes I feel like shooting my brains out and having it over with."

"It's a great life if you don't weaken," said Slim.

"It'll get better," said Al, clapping Bob's shoulder. "Live in hope."

"Let's go," said Jake.

They filed to the detail desk and gave their names and table numbers to a clerk who jotted them down into a huge black ledger, opposite which was inserted the time of day. They had fifteen minutes in which to empty their bowels and bladders and check in again.

"Come on," said Bob, leading the way past windows and tables piled high with mail.

"Gee, it's cloudy out."

"Look like it wants to snow."

"Yeah, it's getting cold again."

The lavatory was full of clerks, black and white. A hot stench of urine and tobacco smoke choked the air. There was a soft murmur of conversation, like a continuous groan. Some clerks sat on stools with the covers down; they had pulled off their shoes and were squeezing sweaty stockinged feet in their hands to ease the pain of standing all day. Others leaned against the walls with half-closed eyes. At the left end of the lavatory, high up in the side of the wall, were the inevitable slits for spying. Other than the entrance door, there was no ventilation, and over the quiet flow of talk rose the never-ending drone of an acre of machines.

Almost ripping his belt loose, Bob made for a commode and flopped down.

"Look, old Bob's got to set down to leak," said Jake.

"Man, you bad's a woman," laughed Al.

"Aw, qqquit rrrazzing 'im," coughed Slim.

Jake watched Bob close his eyes, bite his lips, lean his head back against a wall, and knot his fingers in pain between his legs.

"You know one thing?" said Slim.

"What?"

"That nigger's sick."

"You telling me?"

Jake averted his head, cleared his throat with a deep bellygrunt, and spat a black gob of dust-filled phlegm into a urine commode. He glanced furtively out of the corners of his eyes to see who was smoking; a few were, stealthily. He rushed out his pack of cigarettes, lit one by bending low and cupping his hands, sucked three long draws, snuffed it, and put the butt into his vest pocket. He held the smoke in his lungs as long as he could, hearing the whispering rustle of tissuepaper and the constant gurgle of water. Then he let it eddy slowly through his nostrils. It felt good. He would finish the butt next time. To be caught smoking meant a hundred demerits.

"What place is this where we going tonight?" asked Slim.

"To a joint run by a dame named Rose."

"Where abouts?"

"Over on Calumet."

"Hot spot?"

"That's what I hear."

"Any good meat going to be there?"

"What you think I'm taking you for?"

"I feel like tearing up something tonight."

"Lawd, you sure tore up the last mama you had."

"Boy, that dame said she didn't *never* want to see me no more!"

"You ought to go easy on 'em, Slim."

"Can't help myself, man. The only thing I like better than meat is more meat."

Jake laughed.

Al edged close, buttoning his pants and holding a crumpled newspaper under his arm.

"I see where that Python Killer got the chair," he said.

"Yeah? Let's see."

"Aw, they ain't going to burn her. They'll pardon her just before her time's up."

Al spread the paper and a knot of clerks gathered.

"Jeeesus, she's a hot-looking mama!"

"Now, just look at her! Setting up there smoking that cigarette with her legs crossed!"

"What's she setting on?"

"She's setting on the edge of the bathtub!"

"They say she cut a guy's throat and let the blood run down the drain."

"She killed six men. She drugged 'em and then smothered 'em to death with pillows when they was sleeping."

"But from the looks of that baby I wouldn't mind taking a chance on being smothered at night."

"Boy, if she tried to smother me I'd *show* her some smothering!

"Maybe that was what was wrong with her men. They couldn't *smother* right."

They laughed.

"Yeah, but she was a hardhearted old bitch. She dug holes in her basement and buried the men she killed."

"How in hell could a woman looking that good do things like that?"

"You never can tell. Some of these babies look like sugar but they's poison inside."

"That woman was a bloodsucker."

"Look at the picture of that snake that guy drawed in. Got that snake wrapped around a man's neck."

"That's to show you she was just like a snake. . . ."

". . . a Python."

"And look, here's her face all marked and plotted out."

"What it say?"

"Her eyes is close together, meaning she's mean."

"And her bottom lip pokes out, meaning she's deceitful. She fooled folks."

"And that thick neck? What it say about it?"

"That means," read Al: " 'Uncontrollable passions, masculine feelings.' "

"Gawd, she must've been tough."

"She was tough. She bumped off six men."

"The papers say she got a kink in her brain."

"How that happen?"

"Maybe she fell when she was a baby. . . ."

". . . and bumped her head?"

"You reckon if they smoothed that kink out she'd get all right?"

"How in hell can they do that? They'd have to open up her skull."

"Aw, them papers don't know what they's talking about. Folks is just born to kill, and if they's born to kill, they'll kill, that's all!"

118

"Yeah, you have to do what Gawd's done planned for you to do."

"What's going to happen to you is going to happen."

"And nothing you can do ain't going to help none."

"That reminds me of that Tiger Woman. . . ."

"And the Cat Killer. . . ."

"And the Canary Girl, the one who had the sweet voice and killed all her babies. . . ."

"And them thrill guys, Loeb and Leopold. . . ."

"Aw, it's some strange folks in the world. . . ."

Somebody pulled a chain and water tumbled and droned.

"Let's go," Bob whispered, leaning against a wall, his eyes bloodshot, slowly fastening his belt, his breath coming fast.

"How you feel?" asked Jake.

"I'll be all right in a second, but I hope I don't never have to come in here no more as long as I live. . . ."

"Aw, buck up," said Al, catching Bob's arm. "Ain't nothing as bad's it seems."

Having been out fifteen minutes, they checked in again.

"Jake Jackson."

"Sixty-nine on the small!"

"Robert Madison."

"Seventy on the small!"

"Albert Johnson."

"Seventy-one on the small!"

"Nathan Williams."

"Seventy-two on the small!"

Bentbacked and with their eyes on the dirty steel, they shuffled in the direction of the small letter racks. There were six rows, each row some forty feet long with letter racks on both sides of the row. Each took his place in front of a case. Above their eyes swung an electric bulb with a green shade which deflected a circle of light over the fronts of honeycomblike pigeon-holes. To all four sides were suspended catwalks in which were slits for spying. Midway between their loins and knees was a wooden ledge about twelve inches wide upon which rested their trays of mail. Mingling with the drone of voices and the clatter of machines was the constant sound of rusty steel grating upon rusty steel. Each pigeon-hole was labeled: Texas, Mississippi, Indiana, New York, Rhode Island, California, Michigan, Illinois, Florida. . . . This was known as the Primary Separation, that is, the first separation which the mail underwent when it was brought into the Post Office. Above their heads was a maze of moving belts carrying sorted mail to state sections, and each time a steel tray struck a roller a loud clank was heard. To their rear was a battery of cancelling machines which threw off an odor of hot ink. Every six or seven feet was a rusty spittoon surrounded with sawdust. No mail had as yet come from the cancelling machines and Jake stood with his knee resting upon the ledge.

"MAIL FOR PRIMARY SEPARATION!" a voice bawled.

As one man the line of clerks turned to the right and filed to the end of the aisle. Each picked up a tray of mail and set it upon a scale; its weight was jotted down into a big black ledger.

"Your number?" a clerk asked Jake.

"Sixty-nine on the small," Jake answered.

The weight of each man's mail and the time of day were jotted down opposite the number, and this number referred to his name; hence at any moment it could be told how much work each clerk had done, and what rate of speed. When back at his case, Jake propped his knee again upon the ledge, caught his left hand full of letters, licked his right thumb, and threw letters into the pigeon-holes: Rhode Island—Delaware—Idaho—Maine—Tennessee—Michigan. . . . He paused, cleared his throat, spat, adjusted the green shade on his light, and threw again. He had thrown this separation for so many years that it had become automatic with him. Slim was on his right, wheezing. Bob was to his left, shifting from foot to foot, biting his lips, frowning. Somewhere he heard Al's deep voice droning, laughing, quietly joyous. *That nigger don't never worry.* Sleep hung heavy in his blood and his legs were getting stiff. He remembered the scene in the office when he had stood before the Board. A new hatred against the Negro, Howard, rose up in him. *He just had to put his two cents in! Just to showoff! I'm sure glad old Doc got me out of that jam, if for nothing but to show that black nigger that he ain't the only chicken on the roost. Let 'im wash his face with it, by Gawd!* He remembered still another scene when Howard had hurt his feelings. He had been before the Board and Howard had used the word "Negro" in front of Swanson. *He could've called me colored at least.* It was all right for one Negro to call another Negro "nigger"; but when in front of white folks one ought to be careful. *And that word ain't the same when a white man uses it. There's something he puts in it that ain't right.* And he resented a great many other things like that. When he went to the movies he always wanted to see Negroes, if there were any in the play, shown against the background of urban conditions, not rural ones. Anything which smacked of farms, chain gangs, lynchings, hunger, or the South in general was repugnant to him. These things had so hurt him once that he wanted to forget them forever; to see them again merely served to bring back the deep pain for which he knew no salve.

"CLEAN OUT!"

As he dropped his handful of mail he heard a hundred other hands dropping theirs. He turned to the right again and followed the line of white men and black men who weaved in and out of the long rows of letter racks. Some sentimental thought always made him carry a Northern state rather than a Southern one. He never wanted to carry Mississippi, his home state. *That's one state I'm damn glad to be from.* He held his left arm stiff and straight, pointing floorward, about a foot from his body with the open palm of his hand extended upward. From each Illinois hole he took a handful of mail and stacked it in his left hand until it reached his chin, walking slowly from case to case. When he could take no more, he went to the tray station where he dumped the mail into a large tray, set the metal notch which would guide it to its section, and placed it upon a moving belt. The tray bumped off into the hazy air, clanking over the belt, carrying the mail to state sections where it would be sent to the ends of the world. Jake turned on his heel mechanically and started another cleanout.

"FILL IN!"

He was at his case again, throwing mail.

"I'm going to Jones at swingtime to see if he'll let me have that money," said Jake to Slim. "You want to come with me?"

"Sure."

"You, Bob?"

"O.K."

Another set of clerks was checking in at the Detail Station. Trucksful of dirty, wet mail bags stood in the aisles, waiting to be unloaded and sorted.

"It must be raining or snowing," said Slim.

"It's snowing," said Bob, bending and looking out of a window.

"Here come the gals!" called Al.

A group of about fifteen Negro women was checking in at the Detail Station. Most of them were beyond thirty, having come into the Post Office during the days of the World War when the postal service was undermanned. They were round-shouldered and dumpy-looking, and as they passed in the direction of their detail, white clerks and black clerks turned their heads to look at them.

"Them pale faces sure look at them women like they was bitches," said Jake.

"They got it coming to 'em," said Bob.

"Yeah, let a nigger woman make fifty dollars a week and

121

she begins to think she's too good for her own race," said Jake.

"Aw, forget 'em," said Al.

"I ain't worrying about 'em," said Jake. "But it just makes my blood boil to see a nigger woman grinning at a white man like they do. And these white men around here don't give a good Gawddamn about us. We'll just be clerks as long as we stay here, but they's got a chance to rise as high as a man can go. . . ."

"You right about that," said Slim.

"The race ought to stick together," said Bob.

"You know," said Jake, "the time they caught that nigger woman and that white clerk in the office I was 'shamed to look a white man in the face around here. I felt they was laughing at me."

"I felt the same way myself."

"They look at us like we's dogs anyhow, and when our women ain't got no better sense'n to act like dogs, that makes 'em feel they's treating us right."

"I'd like to horsewhip every black bitch who so much as *looks* at a white man," said Jake.

"You ain't by yourself."

"That reminds me," began Jake. "I. . . ."

"INSPECTION!"

A sudden voice boomed into Jake's ear and made him start. He turned and looked into the red face of a white man. It was the section inspector. Jake sighed, put down his mail, and stepped aside. The inspector went through the cases, examining each hole. Two New York letters were found in the Missouri hole; one Michigan letter was found in the city (Chicago) hole; and four letters bound for Pennsylvania were found in the New Mexico hole. The inspector finished and tapped the eight misthrown letters gently against the letter rack. He looked at Jake a whole minute before he spoke.

"What's the matter, Jackson?"

"Nothing," Jake drawled, trying to smile.

"You think this is something to laugh about, hunh?"

"Naw, sir. I know it ain't. . . ."

"You bet your boots it's not! Now, what's wrong?"

"Ain't nothing wrong."

"You sick?"

"Naw, sir."

"Sleepy?"

"Naw, sir."

"How do you account for these eight misthrown letters?"

"I don't see how in the world it happened," said Jake. "I was working pretty careful. . . ."

"Yeah," sneered the inspector. "You were working carefully, all right! You've been running your mouth like a bluestreak for half an hour! Why don't you quit playing around and do your work!"

Jake's neck grew hot. The inspector had spoken in a loud, harsh voice.

"I'm doing my work," Jake whined, trying to placate the man. "I went to the can a few minutes ago. Somebody must've been working on my case. . . ."

"You're lying! You just came here! I saw you! You haven't been anywhere since you've been on this case," said the inspector, taking out his note book. "I'm going to give you a writeup."

"Do it and quit yelling at me!" Jake snapped.

"Don't give me none of your lip!"

"Don't give me none of *yours*!"

"Who do you think you're talking to!"

"You didn't have to yell at me!"

"I'll talk to you like I damn please!"

"Naw, you wouldn't if you wasn't in here!"

"You *threatening* me!"

"Give me my writeup and quit talking to me!"

"I'm not taking orders from you!"

Jake stepped back and flung his arms wide.

"Why don't you pick on somebody else?"

"Why don't you stop fooling around?"

"I ain't fooling around," said Jake stubbornly.

"Don't this look like it?" asked the inspector, shaking the letters in his face.

Jake trembled. He was conscious that two hundred men had stopped work and were watching him. He knew he was already in bad, and it would not do him any good to face that Board again. He swallowed and made an attempt to get back to his case, but the inspector stepped in front of him, blocking the way.

"Wait a minute! You think you're going to delay the United States mail and get off this easy?"

Jake looked at him with a dogged, fixed stare. He felt his muscles flexing. He was trying to keep from getting mad.

"Look what you've done!" the inspector railed. "Not a man in the whole section can work because of your big lip! You think you're going to get away with *that*?"

"You started it," Jake growled.

"*I* threw those letters wrong, *did* I?" the inspector bellowed.

Something hot engulfed Jake and his head swam. He felt as he had felt that morning when Lil had talked back to him. He heard his voice speaking loudly.

"How come you don't pick on some of them white clerks? How come you always hopping on us colored boys! Gawddammit, I'm sick of this if ain't nobody else is. . . ."

"Aw, come on, Jake!" said Al, grabbing his arm.

"Leave me alone!" Jake bawled.

"It's all right!" said Slim.

"Hush, Jake!" said Bob.

They held him.

"I'm recommending you for two hundred demerits," said the inspector. "You're going to hear from this."

Jake broke from his friends and walked with his head down to the end of the aisle and stood, glowering. *Gawd damn that white bastard's soul!* He did not return to his case until after the inspector had finished, closed his note book, shoved it into his hip pocket, and walked swaggeringly away.

They worked for a while in silence.

"Seems like the white folks just wants to ride a nigger to death," Jake mumbled.

Slim coughed, bending over, holding on to the ledge for support.

"Yeah," he said, between wheezes. "But there ain't nothing a man can do about it."

"You just have to swallow it and like it," said Bob.

"I wanted to push his puss in," said Jake.

"It wasn't you, it was me," said Al.

"And he didn't look at a single case but mine," said Jake. "Shhsh. . . ."

Out of the corner of his eye Jake saw the inspector standing at the end of the aisle, watching. He bent his head lower and threw his mail faster. *You sonofabitch! It ain't always going to be this way!* His mind went abruptly blank. He could not keep on with that thought, because he did not know where that thought led. He did not know of any other way things could be, if not *this* way. Yet he longed for them *not* to be this way. He felt that something vast and implacable was crushing him; and he felt angry with himself because he had to stand it. He had an impulse to whirl and sweep his arm in a wide swift arc and brush away everything. But there was nothing he could solve by doing that; he would only get into more trouble. And the feeling that he could do nothing doubled back upon him, fanning the ashes of other dead feelings of not being able to do anything, and he was consumed in a fever of bitterness.

"Here comes some white piece," whispered Bob.

To his left Jake saw a party of six young white girls coming down the aisle. They were being led by Swanson who stopped now and then to explain the mechanism of the mail to them.

"Ladies, this is the Primary Separation. . . ."

Jake pushed letter after letter into the pigeon-holes, feeling the eyes of the white inspector on him from the end of the aisle, and feeling the eyes of the white women on him from behind. There swept through him a sense of outrage, deep, hot, wild. He was conscious of the sticky sweatstains in the armpits of his shirt, and he felt the edges of his wet BVDs cutting into his loins.

". . . from here the mail is sent to state sections, where. . . ."

The voice was moving on. He heard murmurs of laughter, light, silvery. Through lowered eyes he glimpsed the flash of a flesh-colored ankle. *They's looking at us like we was monkeys in a zoo!* A phrase he had heard an old Negro preacher say down South in his youth welled up in his consciousness, ringing in his ears like a bell. *Lawd, if I had my way I'd tear this building down!* If only there was something he could do to pay the white folks back for all they had ever done! Even if he lost his own life in doing it! But what could he do? He felt the loneliness of his black skin. *Yeah, some foreign country ought to whip this Gawddamn country! Some black country ought to do it!* He remembered the parade he had seen that morning when he was on his way to work. *Yeah, maybe they's right. Who knows?* He saw millions of black soldiers marching in black armies; he saw a black battleship flying a black flag; he himself was standing on the deck of that black battleship surrounded by black generals; he heard a voice commanding: "FIRE!" *Boooooom!* A black shell screamed through black smoke and he saw the white head of the Statue of Liberty topple, explode, and tumble into the Atlantic Ocean. . . . *Gawddamn right!*

He sighed, blinking, pushing a letter for Mississippi through the twelve-inch guns of the black battleship. He was sleepy. And thirsty. He went to the fountain and got a drink; then he held his wrists under the icecold stream of water to chill his blood in order to keep awake. When back at his case he continued building dreams of a black empire. He had reached that point in his imagined epic where black troops were about to conquer the whole world when a metallic gong boomed throughout the Mailing Division, and a voice yelled:

"TWELVE-THIRTY CLERKS CHECKOUT FOR LUNCH!"

There immediately followed the dying moan of many dynamos and the irregular clacking of wheels slackening speed. Jake sighed and turned on his heel with almost a prayer in his heart. *Thank Gawd for that. . . .*

125

III.

"Oh, so you're back again, hunh, Jake?" asked fish-eyed Jones.

"Yes, sir."

Jones toyed reflectively with the inkwell.

"Still looking for dough?"

"I'm still working. It'll be safe with me."

Jones opened the inkwell and peered cautiously inside.

"How bad you want this dough, Jake?"

"I'm on my hind legs," said Jake, grinning.

"How much you want?"

"One hundred iron men."

Jones compressed his lips and pushed the inkwell to a far spot on the desk where he seemed to see it with new objectivity.

"That's a lot of dough, Jake."

"But a hundred's what I want."

"Yeah, but that's a lot of dough."

"Now, look here, Mister Jones, you knows me. Your dough's safe with me. If I don't pay you back you can get a judgement against me."

"Oh, I know that, all right. I believe you'll pay."

"Well, can I get a hundred?"

"I'll sign for 'im," said Slim.

"And I'll sign," said Bob.

Jones lit his cigar, spat a shred of tobacco, and pushed the inkwell farther away.

"It'll cost you twenty dollars, Jake," he said, looking up directly. "I'll have to charge you high because we've let so much money out this week."

Jake hesitated. *Twenty bucks is a lot of dough to pay for a hundred. But I got to get something from somewhere. . . .*

"Well, I reckon that's O.K."

"How long you want it?"

"I'll start paying you back this payday."

"That's the way to talk!"

Jones filled his fountain pen from the inkwell and commenced writing out the form.

"Make it snappy," said Jake. "We ain't got but a half hour to eat in."

"It won't take but a minute."

Jake winked and Bob gave him an answering wink. When the form was all filled out, Slim and Bob attached their names.

126

"Here you are," said Jones, counting out the bills.

"Yes, sir."

"You going to strut your stuff tonight, Jake?" asked Jones.

"I ain't going to do nothing different."

"How about your wife?"

"Oh, yes, sir. . . . I'll have enough left for her. Yes, sir!"

Jones leaned back, chuckled, rolled his cigar from one corner of his mouth to the other, and drummed his long white fingers caressingly upon the tarnished top of the inkwell.

They made a wild dash for the canteen. It was crowded, hot, smoky. They stood in long queues and stamped their feet as the smell of food whetted their hunger. Jake bought cabbage and hamhocks. Bob, sauerkraut and frankfurters. Slim, baked beans and sweet potatoes. Al, pork roast, white potatoes, and ten slices of white bread. Each got a pint milk bottle full of coffee and sweetened it from a huge sugar bowl with a spoon chained securely to the end of a counter. When their trays were filled they placed them on the edges of a table, leaving the center clear so there would be room to play bridge. Bob pulled from his hip pocket a frayed deck of cards; Jake grabbed it and dealt. They arranged their hands, chewing, holding whole slices of bread in their mouths to save the time of lifting a slice for each bite. After they had bid, Slim mumbled through a mouthful of beans:

"Awright, let her go!"

"Here she comes!" sang Al, leading with an ace.

Jake was elated. Now and then he stretched his neck and forced down a half-chewed wad of cabbage. The one hundred dollars nestled compactly in his hip pocket. Only one thing blocked the road to complete freedom; he had four more hours to work. But after that. . . . He flipped down his card to each trick and wagged his head from side to side in tune to an imaginary jazz melody.

"Lawd, I'm going to paint the town red!" he sang.

"I'm going to be the tail on your kite!" sang Al.

"And I'm going to be the shadow on the ground," sang Slim.

"What you going to do, Bob?" Jake asked.

Bob smiled sickly, dealing the second hand. They laughed.

"I'll string along," said Bob. "But I ain't promising I'll do nothing."

"Aw, just looking at a dame won't hurt you none," said Al.

"It's thinking about 'em what hurts," said Bob.

"Keep your mind where your treasure is," sang Al.

They laughed again. At the end of the fourth hand Bob rose and said:

"We got five minutes. I'll meet you guys upstairs."

127

"Take it easy, Bob," said Slim, doubling up with a fit of coughing.

The huge quantity of hot food they had bolted made them drowsy and constricted about the heart. They filed heavily back to the Mailing Division.

"Jake Jackson."

"Machine twenty."

"Robert Madison."

"Machine twenty-one."

"Albert Johnson."

"Machine twenty-two."

"Nathan Williams."

"Machine twenty-three."

Belching and sucking their teeth, they trudged slowly to the cancelling machines and threw the levers; a loud metallic clatter rose and the floor shook beneath their feet. To their right was a long ledge piled high with uncancelled mail. In a little swinging shelf under the edge of each machine was a tiny drawer with metalcut numbers and letters showing the time of day; these numbers and letters had to be inserted in the machine every half hour. Jake adjusted the time on his machine, grabbed a handful of "small" mail and let it run through the narrow slit whose bottom was a moving belt. The mail fluttered out the other end, stacking itself automatically, cancelled. When enough had been run through to fill the container, a carrier carted it off in steel trays. Jake's carrier was a tall, black West Indian Negro, and Jake did not like West Indian Negroes, and especially the tall, black West Indian Negro who was carrying mail off his machine. He was a tight-lipped and thin-lipped fellow who walked about with his head up and his back straight; he never talked much and he held his eyes at an angle that made it seem to Jake he was looking down upon him from some great height. Jake had heard this Negro boast that he had not been born under the Stars and Stripes, but under the Union Jack; that his foreparents had never been slaves, and that he had always been a free man. *And he don't even want to talk like us,* thought Jake bitterly, ramming handful after handful of mail into the machine. *He's got to put a twist on every word. Why in hell they let them bastards come into this country's a mystery to me.* And his dislike for West Indian Negroes made him think of Filipinos. *Them little cute bastards!* He spat into a spittoon. He did not like the straight, slick, black hair of the Filipinos, nor their small mouths, nor their straight noses, nor the smell of the perfume they used. *And they think they's too good to marry a black woman. They got to marry white. Hell, they's colored just like we is!* And he remembered that one of the Filipinos was studying art at the

128

Chicago Art Institute; he had seen him showing his water-colors to white clerks on the job. *Who in hell wants to mess around with stuff like that but a sissy?* And Jake also remembered that last year one of the Filipinos' wives had given Slim a date, and after Slim had seen her once he had to dodge for a week to get the woman off his track. *That just goes to show that them sissies ain't no good. All they fit for is to make some dame ripe for a good man.* He smiled, shooting handsful of mail through the machine. The last image of the white woman tracking Slim down appeased him, and he grew oblivious of the West Indian Negro who carried mail off his machine.

He looked at the clock; only forty-five minutes had elapsed since lunch. *Gawd, how slow the time passes!*

"LISTEN FOR NEW DETAIL!"

Jake held himself ready to hear the hurriedly barked words that were coming. A foreman walked from machine to machine with a pad of paper and pencil poised.

"Jake Jackson," Jake mumbled when the foreman was opposite him.

"Fat stock, hand stamp!"

"Albert Johnson."

"Fat stock, hand stamp!"

"Robert Madison."

"Fat stock, hand stamp!"

"Nathan Williams."

"Fat stock, hand stamp!"

They flicked levers; the machines clattered slowly to silence. The bottoms of their feet tingled when the floor was still. In single file they dragged across the steel again and took places at little individual tables which were piled high with uncancelled mail too thick to be handled by machine. It was called "fat stock". On each table, opposite the elbow, was a black dauber which had inserted in its bottom steel discs to make imprints of post marks. Round black inkpads scented the air with a sharp, fresh smell, like that of raw meat. Jake made sure that his dauber had the correct time of day, and, pulling pieces of mail toward him with his left hand, he began stamping with the dauber, hitting the inkpad and then the stamps on the letters. *Boombomp, boombomp, boombomp, boombomp. . . .* Four licks a second, two hundred forty licks a minute. He paused and wiped his inksmeared thumb on a wad of greasy cotton. He hated hand stamping; there was no way to loaf or talk here. Either he stamped steadily or a foreman bawled. A conflict rose in him. Should he continue hand stamping or check out to the lavatory and rest? He decided to stay; he did not want to risk another quarrel with the foremen; he was in enough trouble already.

129

Then suddenly peace came; he felt tired no longer; his left hand drew the letters toward him and his right hand struck them with the dauber. *Boombomp, boombomp, boombomp, boombomp.* . . . His mind and body had fallen into the rhythm of the thing.

In the faces and attitudes of the clerks the strain of the workday had begun to tell. Limbs moved with increasing listlessness. Slight puffs appeared beneath eyes that looked out with beaten, hang-dog expressions. Crowns of heads were covered with thin layers of dark grey dust. Lips grew stiff and dry from thirst. The spittoons became filled with black mucus. Nervously exhausted from years of racking labor, some worked with spasmodic jerkings of arms and shoulders. Now and then they looked at the clock and sighed from a numbing weariness of spirit. Sometimes images would flit aimlessly into their minds and then aimlessly out again, like stray cats slinking across deserted streets at midnight. Often they were on the verge of speaking, but the sheer triviality of what they wanted to say weighted their tongues into silence. And then, too, talking, no matter of what brand, took a certain amount of energy, energy they were reluctant to spare when hand stamping. During the slow seep of hours their fatigued nerves magnified the sensations of their bodies. They felt their hearts pumping laboriously. Each tingle of the skin was something to be investigated and wondered at. They scratched their scalps, their thighs, their groins, screwing up their eyes in perplexity.

"We's about to catch up with this stuff," said Slim with a sticky throat.

Jake saw that the trough holding the fat stock was nearly empty. When the last piece had been stamped, they stood at the tables and relaxed.

"Lawd, I'm tired!"

"Look like my flesh ain't got no feeling."

"Seem like these last four hours ain't never going to end."

"Ain't it funny how when you was a kid you could play all day and never get tired?"

"Yeah, and now just two hours is enough to poop you out!"

"You know one thing?"

"What?"

"I wouldn't get so damn tired if I knowed where some of this mail was going."

"Some people asking for money to get home, maybe."

"And somebody telling somebody that somebody else is dead, maybe."

"Yeah, maybe a lot of great things in these letters."

"It's hard to just move your hands all day and not see what you doing."

"Like a squirrel turning in a cage."

"This kind of work'll drive a guy nuts."

"I'm thinking he's nuts when he takes a job like this."

"But you got to eat."

"That ain't no lie."

"Sometimes I feel like being just a hobo."

"And never think about nothing."

"If you don't never work you'll come out in the end just about as good as you would if you did work."

"Seems that way."

A foreman rushed up, bawling:

"All through?"

No one answered. The foreman looked into the empty trough and whirled with notebook and pencil poised.

"All right, let's go!"

"Jake Jackson," Jake drawled, tired and slow.

"Fill in on third and fourth class!"

"Robert Madison."

"Third and fourth class!"

"Albert Johnson."

"Third and fourth class!"

"Nathan Williams."

"Third and fourth class!"

They were now out of the division where the first class mail was handled, and away from the rush. They could take it a little easier and talk. They stacked circulars into canvas gurneys, making neat rows. Mail from Sears & Roebuck, Montgomery Ward, Marshall Field. . . .

"Say, Jake?" said Al.

"Yeah?"

"I want to ask you something."

"Shoot."

"You know I been in the National Guard for five years now."

"Yeah, I know."

"How come you won't make up your mind and join us?"

"Aw, I don't know, Al. . . ."

"You ought to, Jake. It's a great life. You just the type of guy we need."

"Aw, I been too busy to think about it," drawled Jake.

"You missing a lot if you don't come in with us. The only thing next to the National Guard is the United States Army, you know."

"Yeah?"

"It ain't in every state we colored folks can join the National Guard."

"Aw, I reckon I'm kind of soft," said Jake, smiling.

131

"One good drill a week'd do you fine. Put some pep into you."

"Oh, I reckon it would."

"And there's that two-week vacation every year with pay. Jake, boy, you don't know what a swell time we have down at Camp Grant. It's a great bunch of fellows. Swimming, boxing, racing. . . . And don't tell nobody, but a little firewater and a dame or two. And Jake, all the officers is colored, just like we is. Say, you'd like it! You'd be wild about it! And listen, how would you like to have a night off every week away from all this damn dust?"

"Sounds good!"

"Nigger, you'd be a better man if you joined up with us," said Al, punching Jake playfully in the ribs.

Jake turned and looked honestly and seriously at Al.

"Tell me, what's this thing for?"

"Ain't nothing to it, Jake. Look, when the Reds start something, we put 'em down, see? If some guys think they can strike and tie up things, we stop 'em, see? If riots break out, we's right on hand, see? Boy, you should have heard the speech the Governor handed us last week. It was a pip! And Jeeesus, you get *paid* for it! And here's something that's right down your alley; when you get into any trouble in the Post Office, they ain't as hard on you as they is when you ain't a soljer. . . ."

"Sure enough?"

"Absolutely, man. You wouldn't've had to pay all that dough out to Doc if you was in the National Guard," said Al. "Our Colonel could've done you some good for nothing."

"Say, that ain't bad at all," said Jake.

"There ain't nothing like it," pronounced Al, chewing a piece of gum. "Come on down with me next week and join. I'll see that you's put in my company. . . ."

"Well, I'll think about it," Jake drawled.

"How come you got to *think* about it? Come on down."

"Naw, not next week."

"Lawd, you sure is one more lazy nigger," said Al, pulling down the corners of his mouth.

"Shucks!" said Slim. "If my lungs was all right I'd join."

"I couldn't pass that shortarm inspection," said Bob.

They laughed.

"Jake's just *lazy*," said Al again, with emphasis.

"I ain't no more lazy than you is," retorted Jake.

"The army'll make a man out of you," said Al.

"Hell, I'm a man already," said Jake.

"That's just what *you* think! A soljer knows how to whip a woman's jelly."

132

"You talk like I don't know how to whip a woman's jelly!"

"You got to prove it to me," said Al.

"I can whip it till the butter comes," said Jake.

They laughed again.

"But not like a soljer," said Al.

"Aw, nigger," said Jake, "whose butter you ever whip to make you brag so?"

"I done whipped more jelly than you, I bet."

"That's a lie!"

"You wouldn't be in all the mess you in now with that dame of yours if you was in the army and knowed how to handle a woman."

"How's that?"

"A soljer never lets a woman get the best of 'im. He knows how to handle 'em."

"I know how to handle 'em," said Jake.

"You *didn't!*"

Jake scratched his head and frowned.

"Aw, I just got a little mixed up with old Lil," he drawled. "Something slipped. . . . I had it all figgered out, and then something went wrong and she had to go and get sick!"

"How's that?" asked Slim.

"What happened?" asked Bob.

"Well, you see," said Jake, "I tricked her into having that first operation. She was just a little dummy when I married her, just seventeen. She would've believed that water wasn't wet if I had told her so. I could have pissed up her back and made her think it was raining. Well, one morning she comes to me all sad and serious, and says she's going to have a baby. At first I tried to get her to go to a quack to get some medicine so she'd pass the damn thing, but she was scared stiff. She had heard of gals dying from them kind of operations and I couldn't get her to move a peg. Then I gets busy and hatches up a smart scheme. I goes to my quack and makes a deal with him; I told 'im to tell her she just couldn't have a baby, that her hips was too little, that she'd die, or just anything as long as she wouldn't have it. Who in hell wants a lot of sticky babies? He put the job over and she was shaking like a leaf; she was between the Devil and the deep blue sea. While the quack was working on her from one end, I was working on her from the other; in no time we had her so she didn't know if she was going or coming. I told her that it would kill her to have that baby, and she went flying down to the quack, begging 'im to pull that damn thing out of her, and do it quick. It cost me five hundred iron men. . . . Boy, them quacks'll gut you if you let 'em. Quacks and mouthpieces get all a postal clerk's money.

Abortions and divorces. . . . But Lawd! When she found out what I done! You see, she didn't take the operation so well and had to go to a hospital. They told her the truth about everything. And what did they do that for? Was she *mad?* She cussed me as long as she could see me! And her health ain't been worth a good Gawddamn since. But the bad part of it is, she won't take my word for nothing now, won't believe a thing I say. . . ."

"Aw," said Al, waving his palm scornfully. "You tried to trick her, all right; but you let her get the best of you even at that. . . ."

"Hell, I couldn't help it if she got sick, could I?"

"Let me tell you how to handle a woman," said Al.

"Come on," said Slim. "Let's hear it."

"This is the way the army teaches you: This is floating power, fourwheel brakes action. You see, she was about ten years older'n me, and was a hash slinger in a 36th Street eatshop. She had a damn good job and was pulling down fifteen bucks a week. Now, she wasn't so awfully good-looking, but she had a shape that was out of the books, and that's the truth, so help me! She was husky and built like a horse; she was a match for any buck. No toothpick guy could keep that baby satisfied, I'm telling you. And man, if she really loved a guy she'd give 'im the kind of love that would make a wildcat squall. And she wasn't half way about it, neither. If she was gone on a guy she'd take 'im and keep 'im up, buy his clothes and cigarettes. She said she wanted all her men to be well rested, and if you could've seen how she eaglerocked them big hams of hers when she walked, you would've knowed just what she meant. Boy, that mama could've loved a whole army of men and had plenty of love to spare.

"Well, this is how it all happened. It was easy's pie. In fact, she's the one what did all the running, 'cause I didn't want her at first. Every time I went to the joint to eat supper she'd invite me to her place. I went up a few times and she piled my plate so high with greens, fat meat, and egg cornbread I couldn't eat it all. I knowed she was trying to snare me, but I knowed that a lot of other guys had done had her, and I wasn't so hot on taking secondhand goods, see?

"Then all of a sudden my shift in the stockyards shut down. It was in the dead of the winter and wasn't nothing going on, so I picks up this dame like a hundred carat diamond.

"Boy, did she swipe home some good eats from that eat-shop! It makes my mouth water enough to spit just to think about it. She would come in at night all loaded down like a two-legged express company and start pulling grub out of her bosom and bloomers, and before you knowed it the table'd just be covered with hams, cakes, pies, pigtails, hog's head, chitterlings, pork chops, steaks, roasts, chickens, greens. . . . Lawd, today!

"But she was a funny woman; maybe if it hadn't been for all them freakish ways of hers I would've been with her yet. At first I just couldn't make out what made her act so screwy. Today she'd act like a lamb, and tomorrow she'd be a regular red-hot hyena.

"Well, this is the way she'd act. She'd come in and unload all the grub she'd done swiped, and then start cussing. And did that baby know some cuss words? When she opened up the air'd jump around your head. And she'd start about just any old thing, so no matter what you did you could never tell just where she'd break out. Maybe I'd forgot to put my dirty shirt in the old clothes bag, and she'd ask me: 'Is you a pig?' And right away I'd tell her: 'Naw, Darling. I'll move it right now.' But that wouldn't satisfy that baby none. One word would lead to another and before you knowed it we was in the biggest kind of fuss.

"One night while we was fussing she said: 'And what does you do? I works hard all day and you just sets on your can, doing nothing!' 'Well, baby,' I says, 'I'm willing to work, you know.' 'Like hell you is!' she yells. 'I don't want no tired mens sleeping with me in the bed at night!'

"Man, the whole mess had me so I didn't know my head from my feets. One night after supper when we was fussing I says to her: 'Listen, baby, let's call it quits.' Boy, she broke down and cried like a fool. 'I loves you better'n any man I ever had!' she tells me. 'Don't leave me, Daddy Darling, please. . . .' Well, I stayed, but the very next night she started all over again.

"One night when there was about a foot of snow piled up on the ground, we had a howling big fuss. Even if I didn't have nowhere to go, I was getting good and sick of her by this time, and I stood up for my rights. 'Listen here, you catty bitch!' I says, 'either you close your trap or I'll smack you to a low gravy!' Boy, her hair stood up on end! She dropped the smoothing iron she was ironing with and tore at me like a Bengal tiger and started clawing my face like all hell. 'How's that for a catty bitch?' she asks me.

"Now get this straight. I ain't no man what goes around fighting women, see? But what happened that night just couldn't be helped. I figgered I had done taken about enough off her already. So right then and there I gives her two ringing, sounding slaps that sends her reeling into a corner, squalling bloody murder. She stays on her knees awhile with her face in her hands, moaning. Then all of a sudden she

135

comes at me again. This time I means business; I grabs both of her hands in my left hand and slaps her till she slobbers. She opens up her mouth, clouds up her eyes, and begins to rain tears like all outdoors, begging and pleading with me: 'Don't hit me no more, Daddy Darling, please. . . .'

"The funny thing about it all was she got soft and chummy with me after that. For about a week everything was peaches and roses. Then she started again. I beat her again. You see, I had done found her soft spot. Man, that woman just craved for men to beat her. When she'd come in at night all washed-out from standing on her feets all day and feeling in the dumps from bending over a red-hot stove, there wasn't nothing in all the world better'n being beat black and blue till she forgot all about her tiredness and could cuddle up in my arms for a little love. . . .

"I left her about three months after that. Slipped off and didn't leave no word. I was tired and sick of her, fedup. And anyhow, I had done started losing weight from too damn much exercise. . . ."

Jake, Slim, and Bob bent over the table with laughter.

"Wooooooow!" Jake spluttered. "You sure had her number!"

"It's all in knowing how," said Al. "They learn you that in the National Guard."

"Nigger, you crazy!"

"No kidding, now. Come on down and join up with us, Jake."

"Well. . . ."

"You'll like it."

"Not this week, anyhow."

"Then next week?"

"Wwwell . . . er. . . . Aw, yeah, I'll sign up next week."

"Man, let me shake your hand," said Al, grabbing Jake.

Jake straightened his face in hard, serious lines and spoke with deep gravity:

"It ain't a bad idea to have a gun in your hand when trouble breaks out."

A loud laugh made them turn around. A white clerk stood, watching and listening. Jake, Al, Slim, and Bob stared at him without smiling.

"Gee, that was some hot story," said the white clerk. "Let's hear another one."

Wordlessly, they turned away. A minute passed. They heard the footsteps of the white clerk dying away on the steel floor.

"Can you beat that?" asked Slim.

"That sonofabitch!" spat Al.

"They never want to have nothing to do with us, but when

136

we's talking about women they's always sticking their damn noses in," said Bob.

"Yeah, a white bastard's always thinking we never talk about nothing but that," said Jake.

They were silent, resentful, hurt.

IV.

Directly behind them a window framed a square portion of the evening's flying snow. The wind, rising and dying, howled like a lost dog in a vast wilderness. They stacked batches of mail carefully on the table, pressed them together firmly, and carried them slowly to gurneys. When they grew tired like this, when most of their workday preoccupations had been drowned in exhaustion, their basic moods would blend and fuse. They had worked in this manner for so many years that they took one another for granted; their common feelings were a common knowledge. And when they talked it was more like thinking aloud than speaking for purposes of communication. Clusters of emotion, dim accretions of instinct and tradition rose to the surface of their consciousness like dead bodies floating and swollen upon a night sea.

"Lawd, I'm tired. . . ."

". . . and sleepy. . . ."

". . . I could curl up and snooze till the cows come home."

"Ain't it funny how dopey you feel after you done downed a big meal?"

"It puts you on the bum."

"Makes your legs feel like lead."

"I can't hardly hold my eyes open."

"That's 'cause we ate too much. . . ."

". . . and can't get no fresh air."

"Sleep's a queer thing."

"It's next to being dead."

"It just comes down on you all at once. . . ."

". . . and then you got to sleep."

"A man can't do without sleep."

"You spend a third of your life sleeping."

"You know, I never thought of that."

"But going to sleep's the funny thing."

"Lawd, I like going to sleep."

"It's like slipping off into nothing."

"You ever remember going to sleep?"

"Naw."

137

"You get in the bed sleepy and tired. . . ."

". . . and the first thing you know it's morning. . . ."

". . . and all the time you's sleeping your heart keeps right on beating. . . ."

". . . and you living and ain't thinking about living at all."

"Sort of scares you when you think about it."

"Yeah, it makes you shaky when you think how little stands between you and death."

"Death's an awful thing!"

"No matter how hard you try to figger it out. . . ."

". . . it's something you just can't get use' to. . . ."

". . . and a man'll go nuts just wondering about it."

"Look like you ought to have more'n *one* chance at dying. . . ."

". . . like them cats that got nine lives."

"Yeah."

"Wouldn't seem so bad, then."

"Naw."

"But you can never have a chance like that."

"Never!"

"I can't see head or tail in the whole damn thing!"

"It's just there and you think and think and think. . . ."

". . . and cold chills run up and down your spine."

"But you know, when I sleep I like to dream."

"Me too."

"What makes dreams?"

"Stumps me."

"Some folks say dreams is warnings and if you watch 'em you can tell what's going to happen."

"Yeah, that's what the guys in the Bible did. . . ."

". . . old Noah. . . ."

". . . and Jacob. . . ."

". . . and David."

"But some dreams can scare you."

"Yeah, Lawd!"

"Ever dream you was falling. . . ."

". . . and wake up and find yourself sweating?"

"Lots of times."

"I dreamed about steps last night."

"Gee, I had a funny dream. I thought I was trying to put out a building that was on fire."

"I dreamed about a river, a big, slow moving, deep river. There was a boat running down the middle of it all piled high with cotton."

"I dreamed I was out in the woods hunting, just shooting a gun. *Blooom! Blooom! Blooom!*"

"But I don't like to dream about dead folks!"

"Hell, naw!"

"Say, you ever see a ghost?"

"Plenty times!"

"Shucks, I saw one walk right into a brick wall once, and then I couldn't see 'im."

"Jeeesus!"

"What you do?"

"Hell, I run!"

"I saw something that beats that. We lived in a house once where a door slammed all night long, opening and shutting. They say a whore was murdered in there."

"Aw, that ain't nothing. We lived in a house once where we heard somebody walking around our bed every night, *bomp! bomp! bomp! bomp!*"

"What youall do?"

"We moved out of there real quick!"

"Aw, I done seen something ain't none of youall never seen. I was walking along a road down South one night and saw a man with no head on. . . ."

"With no *head* on?"

"With *no* head on."

"Ain't that a bitch!"

"Wasn't you scared?"

"I couldn't move."

"Where he go?"

"Well, I turned around to look and he was gone. . . ."

"Gone?"

"Gone, man."

"Shucks, I *never* want to see nothing like that!"

"You know, I once heard a guy say your body changes every seven years."

"Yeah?"

"How's that?"

"I don't know. You just change all over and you's still the same guy."

"Look like you ought to change into somebody else."

". . . don't it?"

"There's sure a lot of queer things going on in the world."

"Life's a funny thing."

"Say, take a look at this!"

"What?"

"Here's a piece of mail sent out by a guy what calls himself Saint Paul. . . ."

"Read it!"

"Here, you read it, Al!"

"Look! Two trains, all loaded with people. One train's heading for Heaven and the other's heading for Hell. . . ."

"Who's that over there?"

139

"That's the Devil with a pitchfork."
"And what's that?"
"That's his tail curling round and round."
"Lawd, today!"
"And who's that other guy?"
"That's Jesus. . . ."
"And what's that he's got?"
"He's holding a snow-white lamb in his arms."
"And look at all them white angels. . . ."
". . . and the people. . . ."
". . . millions of 'em!"
"Read the thing!"

WHICH RAILROAD WILL YOU TAKE????????????
****

THE EVERLASTING DAMNATION RAILWAY
CORPORATION
****

The Quickest and Shortest Route to the Hottest Depths
of
HELL
# # # # # # # #
MUCH TIME AND MANY MILES SAVED BY THIS ROUTE
AND YOU WILL ENJOY TERRIFICALLY EVIL SCENERY
EVERY TORTUOUS MILE OF THE
W A Y
. . . .

THIS TRAIN STOPS AT THE FOLLOWING POINTS WEST:
South through Dismal Swamp; Southwest through Murderer's
Gap; Allnight Stopover at Hangman's Gorge; East through Doubt
Thoroughfare; North through Skeptical Valley; and passing
through the following cities: Fire and Brimstone Metropolis,
Pleasure Harbor, Saint Haughty, Atheistville, Infidel City, Fort
Worldly, Sinburg, New Trespassing, Evilsford, Dishonor Island,
Sciencedale, Temptation Mound, Radical Hill, Prideston, Liars-
port, and Whiskey Terminal.
00000000000000000
REACHING THE GREAT VALLEY OF THE SHADOW OF
ETERNAL DEATH AT BLACK MIDNIGHT AND PLUNG-
ING ITS PASSENGERS INTO THE BOTTOMLESS PITS OF
EVERLASTING WOE!!!!!!!!!

M A I N   D E P O T :
Corner Unbelief and Disobedience Streets

ALL HOURS OF THE DAY AND NIGHT SPECIAL TRAINS
ARE RUNNING FROM:

Thomas Paine Avenue, Dime Novel Park, Theatre Lane, Dopedel,
Blasphemers' Hall, Smokers' Furnace, Masturbation Alley, Prosti-
tution Boulevard, Dancehall Station, Highball Lagoon, Adultery
Depot, Greed Mountain, Gambling Pause, Ingersoll Canyon,
Evolution Grounds, and Communist Junction.
****

LIGHTNING SPECIALS FROM SUICIDE AVENUE AT ALL
HOURS!!!!!!!!
****

EXTRA TRAINS AND SPECIAL COACHES
ON SUNDAYS AND HOLIDAYS!
ALL ABOARD!

FARE: THY SOUL
PRINCE LUCIFER, *President.*

"Turn it over. . . ."
". . . and see what it says on the other side."
"This stuff makes your flesh creep."
"You reckon anybody ever do *all* them things?"
"Look at all that fire. . . ."
". . . and smoke. . . ."
". . . and them little black imps!"
"Hell's a terrible place!"
"It must be awful to burn and burn. . . ."
". . . forever and ever. . . ."
". . . and not ever burn up!"
"Boy, the guy what drawed that picture sure knowed what
he was doing."
"Come on, Al, read the other side!"

WHICH RAILROAD WILL YOU TAKE?????????????
,,

THE SALVATION AND REDEMPTION RAILWAY
COMPANY, INC.!!!!
****

RUNNING DAILY FROM THE BLACK VALE OF SINFUL
TEARS TO THE GLORY GATES OF THE GREAT
BEYOND!!!!!!!!!!!!!!!

V I A

Resurrection Mound, Christian Hill, Baptism Vale, Conversion Junction, Contrite Soul Terminal, Mount Calvary, Rugged Cross, Rock of Ages, River of Life, New Jerusalem, Paradise Garden, Everlasting Happiness, Daily Prayer, Sacrifice Harbor, Temperanceville, Honesty Line, and Repentance Lane.

T H R O U G H
THE VALLEY OF THE SHADOW OF DEATH
BY BROAD DAYLIGHT!

00000000000000000

STOPPING AT THE FOLLOWING POINTS:

Meditation Valley, Crucifixion Canyon, Faith Bend, Hope Lagoon, Charity Station, Holy Vineyards, Temple of Joy, River of Milk and Honey, Gates of Saint Peter, Peaceport, Prosperityburg, Blissdom, Sanctuary Town, Pentecostal Depot, Grace Boulevard, Glory Park, Angel City, and Fort Love. STRAIGHT TO THE GRAND CENTRAL DEPOT OF THE UNIVERSE IN THE CITY OF GOD WITHOUT A CHANGE OF CARS!!!!!!!!!!!!!

TRAINS AT ALL HOURS OF YOUR LIFE!!!!!

M A I N   D E P O T :
Corner Faith and Repentance Streets
ALL CARS ARE FIRST CLASS————NO HALF FARES!!!!!!
(No Excursion Tickets! No Round Trip Tickets! No Passes! And No Stopovers!)

THESE TRAINS ARE NEVER LATE
AND LEAVE RIGHT UP TO THE VERY
H O U R   O F   D E A T H

ALL ABOARD!

Jesus Christ, *President*

"You know one thing? Folks is sure getting smart these days."

"They's getting weaker and wiser."

"They's done figgered out every *single* thing."

"They's done mapped out things so plain that even a fool couldn't go wrong if he wanted to."

142

"Some folks say that shows that the end of time ain't far off."

"Yeah, Gawd might get tired of folks wanting to know too much and end everything."

"But Gawd sure must've been with the guy to make 'im write a thing like that."

"He must've showed 'im a vision."

"Man, Gawd's work's a mystery!"

"I reckon that old song's right what says you'll understand it better bye and bye."

"You just can't figger out Gawd's plans. . . ."

". . . and there ain't no use trying."

"Gawd works in a funny way. . . ."

". . . His wonders to perform."

"You know, my ma use' to say that all the time."

"Ain't it funny how somebody can map out the *whole* life of the *whole* world—like Gawd did. . . ."

". . . and make all them trees and flowers and birds. . . ."

". . . and make people and put the breath of life in 'em. . . ."

". . . and set it all to running and spinning. . . ."

". . . like some kind of machine. . . ."

". . . and know everything what's going to happen before it happens?"

"You just can't help wondering how it all got started. . . ."

". . . and how come it was all started. . . ."

". . . and why is everything so big. . . ."

". . . so big you's lost in it. . . ."

". . . that moon. . . ."

". . . them clouds. . . ."

". . . and that sun. . . ."

". . . a big ball of fire. . . ."

". . . and all them miles and miles of empty sky. . . ."

". . . and them stars!"

"It makes your head swim!"

"Scares you just to think about it."

"Jeeesus, all this must of been made for *some*thing."

"Yeah, it couldn't've all been made for *no*thing."

"Funny how some fools can stand up and say there *ain't* no Gawd."

"Ain't it though?"

"They ought to know *some*body must've started all this."

"It couldn't start by it*self*."

"Nobody but a *fool* couldn't see that."

"That's right."

"That's right, all right."

"But Gawd lets some folks in on a lot of secrets. Like old Edison. . . ."

"He was a wizard!"

"They called 'im a genius."

"He invented the 'lectric light. . . ."

". . . and made the lightning work just like a man plows a horse."

"White folks *al*ways inventing something."

"They's smart."

"The white folks do everything so easy. . . ."

". . . working together like a army. . . ."

". . . marching to war!"

"Sometimes when I think about it I almost hate myself."

"Yeah, sometimes I wish I was anything but a nigger."

"We don't stick together."

"If three niggers is trying to do something, one of 'em's going to trip the others up. . . ."

". . . sell 'em out. . . ."

". . . to the white folks. . . ."

". . . like a Judas!"

> *"Niggers is evil*
> *White folks too*
> *So glad I'm a Chinaman*
> *I don't know what to do. . . ."*

"Yeah, the white folks always work and plot together. . . ."

". . . that's why they runs the world."

"The papers say old Edison and Ford was big friends."

"They was what you call successful men."

"You know, I was reading in the papers the other day how all great men started out poor. . . ."

". . . some of them even lived in log cabins. . . ."

". . . and most of 'em was Christians, too. . . ."

". . . like old Benjamin Franklin. . . ."

". . . and old Abe Lincoln. . . ."

". . . and old Rockefeller."

"They got to be successful by following the Golden Rule."

"Yeah, they did to other men what they wanted them men to do to them. . . ."

". . . and Gawd rewarded 'em."

"You'll get your reward if you do right."

"Gawd sees to that. He's done figgered out all kind of ways to reward folks."

"And He can punish you, too."

"Oh, yeah."

"I heard tell of lightning killing a little girl 'cause she said she didn't believe in Gawd."

"And I heard tell of a man who went blind 'cause he laughed at a blind man."

144

"When I was a boy my grandma told me about a man who killed a hunchback. He went to sleep and the next morning he woke up with a hunch in *his* back."

"Gawd'll sure settle with you if you don't do right, now."

"Yeah, He evens up everything."

"Sometimes Gawd waits 'til you's on your deathbed and then He makes you pay."

"Yeah; a real black guy lived in our town down South and he was evil as sin. When he come to die it took 'im a week. He just laid there on his deathbed and screamed and howled. He couldn't eat or sleep. He said a fat hog was standing by his bed with a letter for 'im in his feets. . . . You know, the hog had the letter in his hooves. . . ."

"Have mercy, Lawd!"

"Gawd was punishing that man!"

"You telling me?"

"But Gawd can reward you, too."

"Yeah, remember that guy Wrigley what made millions of dollars just selling chewing gum?"

"And that English guy what made a lot of money selling tea? What was his name?"

"Lipton, wasn't it?"

"That's him."

"And when he got to be a old man he spent his last days trying to win a silver cup by racing boats. . . ."

"He did?"

"Yeah, it was in the papers."

"Shucks, we use' to play that when we was kids."

"Lawd, that must be a good way to live!"

"Nothing to think about but sport. . . ."

"Just live. . . ."

". . . from day to day. . . ."

". . . and have pleasure. . . ."

". . . eating. . . ."

". . . sleeping. . . ."

". . . women. . . ."

". . . everything you want. . . ."

". . . and nothing to worry about."

"Yeah, like them big time baseball players."

"You know, some of them big league players make *fifty thousand* dollars a year."

"Lawd, what would I do with fifty thousand dollars?"

"That's more money than a man can think about."

"A sporting life's a easy life. . . ."

". . . a sweet life."

"Talking about sports . . . I see where the Cubs is busting up their team, throwing away all the bum players."

"Yeah, we ought to have some hot baseball in the National League next year."

"Old Wrigley's trying to buy up a pennant-winning outfit."

"Aw, I don't like them Cubs. Give me the Sox any day."

"Aw, the Cubs is all right."

"How can they be all right when the Sox beat 'em every year in the city series?"

"That don't mean nothing. The Cubs done won the pennant in the National League more times than the Sox done won it in the American."

"But that don't prove a thing! That just goes to show that the American League's tougher than the National!"

"Like hell it do! Some of the best pitchers in the world's in the National League!"

"Pitching ain't *every*thing! *Hitting's* what counts! And the American League's got the hitters!"

"But look at how many games the Cubs done *won!* When you count 'em all up, you'll see they done won *more'n* the Sox!"

"But against *who?*"

"The National League!"

"Aw, *any*body can lick them hicks!"

"You got a grudge against the Cubs, that's all!"

"Gawddamn right! They don't want no colored folks out at Wrigley Field. The white folks throwed a pop bottle at me one day."

"But that ain't no reason to be against the Cubs."

"Why the hell ain't it? I'm against *any*body what's against *me!*"

"Aw, them white folks don't know you alive!"

"Don't care if they don't. I don't like them Cubs!"

"What to hell! How come we can't stand up for our own race? We got some baseball players that's just as good as they got. Who wants to go around whooping it up for the white folks all the time when we got our own stuff?"

"Well, that *is* right. We got old Joe Louis and there ain't never been nobody like him."

"Lawd, it sure made me feel good all the way down in my guts when old Joe socked Baer."

"I said to myself, let them white folks *chew* that."

"When that radio said that Joe'd done won, I jumped up and flew out into the street. I didn't know *where* I was going!"

"Man, I felt like leaping a mile high in the air and just screaming!"

"Just think now. . . . He marries a gal, goes into the ring the same day, and knocks a guy coocoo!"

"You know how come old Joe Louis done that?"

"Naw."

146

"Why?"

"Well, old Joe got in that ring that night with his hair all slicked back and old Baer didn't have no better sense'n to ruffle it. Old Joe just cocked his left and knocked his block off. . . ."

"Hohohoho!"

"Hahahaha!"

"Nigger, you crazy!"

"But old Joe oughtn't've married that dame."

"Hell, naw!"

"That woman'll make 'im weak."

"Damn right."

"You know a woman ruined old Samson."

"Oh, Joe's young yet. . . ."

". . . maybe he'll get use' to it."

"Lawd, I hope so."

"And I'll *never* believe as long as I live that old Joe lost to Schmeling fair."

"Aw, he was doped."

"He could've whipped old Schmeling with one hand if he hadn't been doped."

"The white folks tricked 'im."

"They giving Joe the same old screwing they gave Jack Johnson."

"The white folks just ain't going to let no black man get to the top."

"Naw; just when you think you's nearly there they's done tripped you up."

"You see, they think if they let *one* black man rise that high, then *all* the rest of the black folks'll want to rise."

"Yeah, the white folks'll treat *one* black man all right, but when it's more'n one they gets hard."

"They's scared. . . ."

". . . and mean."

"Aw, boy, they's watching us."

"Shucks, I believe my soul old Joe can lick *any*body!"

"Yeah, but he ain't as good as old Jack Johnson."

"The hell he ain't!"

"He couldn't've *touched* old Jack with a glove!"

"And Jack couldn't've touched *him* neither!"

"Jack was the greatest *defensive* fighter that ever was!"

"And Joe's the greatest *hitter* that ever was!"

"But how can you knock a man out when you can't *hit* 'im?"

"But Joe's a *counter*puncher! Soon's Jack'd try to hit 'im, Joe'd *kill* 'im!"

"Look, see? This is the way old Joe stands, with his left hand high. . . ."

"And this is the way old Jack stands, ready for 'im. . . ."

"All right, now. . . . You lead. . . ."

"All right."

"See!"

"Hell, wait a minute!"

"Old Joe would've done socked 'im *right* on the chin!"

"Nigger, you crazy! Jack would've *ducked* that!"

"Aw, you don't know nothing!"

"I wonder who would've won if them two could've got together? I mean old Joe like he is now and old Jack when he was in his prime. . . ."

"That's hard to tell."

"Lawd, but it would've been a *fight*, though!"

"You telling me?"

"Boy, I want to see just *one* fight like that before I die!"

"I bet you Joe'll never be champion."

"How come?"

" 'Cause the white folks is scared it'll stir up riots all over the country."

"Yeah, I like to hear 'em tell about how folks acted when old Jack beat old Jim Jeffries. . . ."

"You know, they say down South the day Jack Johnson beat Jim Jeffries a nigger walked into a white cafe and asked the white bartender: "Say, white man, give me a cup of coffee strong and black as Jack Johnson and a beef steak all beat up bleeding and red like Jim Jeffries."

"Wooooooooow!"

"What happened?"

"They mobbed that bastard!"

"Jeeesus Christ!"

"Well, I heard a story that said old Jack was driving down Michigan Boulevard in Chicago in his high-powered Packard and a cop arrested 'im for speeding. When they brought him before the judge the judge said: 'Fifty dollars!' Well, old Jack just reached down in his jeans and hauled out a hundred dollar bill and said: 'Keep it all, Judge! I'm going back at the same rate of speed!' "

"Lawd, today!"

"A man's on top when he can do a thing like that!"

"Old Jack was a dog!"

"Aw, folks'd fight about Jack."

"Yeah, that's the trouble, they did too much fighting."

"Them race riots they had just about drove 'im out of the ring."

"A riot's a terrible thing."

"I came to Chicago just two weeks before that big riot they had."

"The white folks was killing up niggers like flies."

"The hell they was! The newspapers said we got the worst of it, but we *didn't.*"

"There was *five* white folks killed for every *black* man."

"You see, the white folks try to make us believe we got the worst of it so's we'll be scared. . . ."

"Yeah, they doing everything to beat us down."

"I remember when that riot started. . . ."

". . . right down on 31st Street. . . ."

". . . on the lake beach. . . ."

". . . one summer day. . . ."

". . . and the white folks stoned a little black boy and drowned 'im 'cause he was swimming in the wrong part of the lake."

"Now, ain't that a bitch! Swimming in the *wrong* part of the lake. . . ."

". . . and the lake is *miles* big."

"That's as bad as killing a man for breathing."

"I wonder is there anything a white man won't do?"

"They make us live in one corner of the city. . . ."

". . . like we was some kind of wild animals. . . ."

". . . then they make us pay anything they want to for rent. . . ."

". . . 'cause we can't live nowhere but where they tell us!"

"I remember when they use' to run us out of our homes with bombs."

"Even when you's dead, they tell you where to go."

"Lawd, today! Jim Crow *graveyards!*"

"Ain't *that* a bitch!

"Who in hell can a *dead* black man hurt?"

"Maybe a black spirit'll rape a white spirit."

"Aw, nigger, hush!"

"Hohohoho!"

"Hahahaha!"

"You know, down South when a black man goes into a white store to buy a cigar he has to say: 'Mister, please give me one of them *Mister* John Ruskin cigars. . . .' Hahaha!"

"They make you drink your milk with bluing in it. . . . Hehehe!"

"They don't allow no *white* hen to lay no *black* eggs, or *black* hens to lay *white* eggs. . . . Hohoho!"

"They make the colored folks dye the sheets on their beds *black!* Hahaha!"

"They kill a *black* cow if she gives white milk. . . . Hehehe!"

"Nigger, hush! Hahaha!"

"Well, it might sound like a joke, but Gawd knows it almost the truth!"

"It wasn't no joke when all them folks was dying in the streets in that riot."

"I seen a black guy take a white man and club his brains out in that riot."

"I heard a man say he saw a black guy slash a white streetcar conductor from ear to ear."

"It's bad luck for a black man anywhere."

"There's somebody always after you, making you do things you don't want to do."

"You know, the first time I ever set down beside a white man in a streetcar up North, I was expecting for 'im to get up and shoot me."

"Yeah, I remember the first time I set down beside a white woman in a streetcar up North. I was setting there trembling and she didn't even look around."

"You feel funny as hell when you come North from the South."

"I use' to walk around all day feeling like I done forgot something."

"Yeah, every time I'd see a white man I'd feel like getting off the sidewalk to let 'im pass, like we had to do in the South."

"It took me a long time to get use' to feeling what freedom was like."

"Ain't it funny how some few folks is rich and just millions is poor?"

"And them few rich folks owns the whole world. . . ."

". . . and runs it like they please. . . ."

". . . and the rest ain't got nothing?"

"Well, you know Gawd said the poor'll be with you always. . . ."

". . . and He was right, too."

"Some folks just ain't got no brains, that's all. If you divided up all the money in the world right now we'd be just where we is tomorrow."

"But don't you think all the white folks is smart. Some of 'em's crazy! I saw in the papers the other day where some old white woman over in Paris said a rose is a rose is a rose is a rose. . . . She wrote it in a book and when they asked her what it was she wouldn't tell. . . ."

"Wouldn't tell?"

"Wouldn't tell, man."

"Jeeesus, that sounds like old Cab Calloway."

"Aw, hell, he ain't never said nothing that crazy."

"But man, the smartest white guy I ever seen was Big Bill Thompson."

"That guy wasn't scared of *no*body!"

150

"Yeah, that old *Chicago Tribune* sure hated 'im 'cause he give the colored folks so much."

"I heard old Big Bill say once that he'd do more for the colored folks if the other white folks'd let 'im."

"Yeah, they was hard on 'im 'cause he was our friend."

"Say, didn't he build a big school for us?"

"I don't know."

"He did something for us 'cause everybody says he did."

"Yeah, but I can't remember what he did."

"Me neither."

"He was a great man. . . ."

". . . something like old Teddy Roosevelt who carried a big stick and talked soft. . . ."

". . . and this other Roosevelt's just like 'im."

"But that old Wilson was a tricky bastard!"

"He tried to mess this country up. . . ."

". . . by getting us in all that war."

"Yeah, when they find out the truth about that guy I'll bet you he was a Red!"

"He wanted all the nations to get together. . . ."

". . . and that's just what the *Tribune* says the Reds want."

"They say a Red's international."

"What's international?"

"Damn if I know."

"Some folks say Roosevelt's a Red."

"But he ain't international."

"How you know?"

"Well, nobody knows just what these white folks is up to."

"But, boy! That guy over in Roosia! That Leenine. . . ."

". . . he was a dog!"

"He scared the piss out of them rich white folks!"

"And they scared *yet!*"

"Boy, he tricked 'em!"

"You ever see his picture?"

"Yeah; all that beard. . . ."

". . . and them eyes. . . ."

". . . and that mouth all screwed up. . . ."

". . . like he could bite nails. . . ."

". . . and that chin turned up in the air."

"Lawd, that man must've been weaned on vinegar!"

"And them eyebrows of his'n. . . ."

". . . going straight up. . . ."

". . . like a Chink's."

"I'll bet you when they find out about 'im they'll find he had some Chink blood in 'im."

"Maybe that was why he was so sly and could fool 'em all."

"He must've had something!"

"And his old pal. . . ."

"What was his name?"

"Tricksky, wasn't it?"

"Something like that. But was he hardboiled? With that hair all flying. . . ."

". . . and them eyes that looked like they could see through you."

"I saw in the paper where they run 'im out of Roosia. He was too hot for them Reds even."

"I heard a Jew boy say that guy wanted a revolution that went on always. . . ."

"*Al*ways?"

"*Always*, man!"

"What kind of revolution's that?"

"Damn if I know."

"Gawddamn, I'm scared of them kind of folks."

"Yeah, everybody's scared of them guys."

"The Reds sure scared them white folks down South when they put up that fight for the Scottsboro boys."

"The American white man is a natural born coward."

"You know one thing, if somebody ever started in on these white folks in honest, you could run 'em square into the ocean."

"They ain't never come up against nothing hard yet."

"And the first time they do they's going to mess all over themselves."

"A white man wouldn't fight you fair for nothing."

"He gangs you."

"And once they get you down they don't have no mercy."

"Look like it's fun to them to see people suffer."

"That's cause they ain't happy. . . ."

". . . and they take it all out on you."

"That's the reason why we had to get out of the South. . . ."

". . . and stop slaving for them white folks from 'kin 'til can't. . . .' "

". . . from sunup to sundown. . . ."

". . . rain or shine. . . ."

". . . picking cotton 'til your back feels like it's going to break in two. . . ."

". . . and that sun so hot you can't even sweat. . . ."

". . . and hoeing 'til your hands blister. . . ."

". . . and plowing. . . ."

". . . shucking corn. . . ."

". . . killing hogs. . . ."

". . . cooking molasses. . . ."

". . . hauling logs. . . ."

". . . laying them railroad ties. . . ."

". . . swinging that hammer. . . ."

152

". . . to drive them hard, hard steel spikes!"

"Gawd, when you think of all the work we black folks done done. . . ."

". . . and ain't got a damn thing to show for it all. . . ."

". . . but bent backs and weak minds. . . ."

". . . you feel like going outdoors and looking up at the sun and cussing Gawd!"

> *"A naughts a naught*
> *A figger's a figger*
> *All for the white man*
> *None for the nigger. . . ."*

"It's the truth!"

"Gawd knows it is!"

"There ain't nothing worse'n a Southern white man but two Southern white men. . . ."

". . . and the only thing worse'n two Southern white men is two Southern rattle snakes!"

"But some of the white folks in the South's pretty good."

"Yeah, the rich ones."

"That's 'cause they got money to live on and don't have to worry."

"But the poor white man's death to a poor black man."

"They grudge you the ground you stand on."

"They's the ones what lynch and burn us."

"Crackers!"

"Rednecks!"

"Hillbillies!"

"And don't they look awful. . . ."

". . . with them old bleached-out blue eyes. . . ."

". . . sunk way back in their heads. . . ."

". . . and that old dead stringy hair. . . ."

". . . falling down over their faces. . . ."

". . . like a dirty mop. . . ."

". . . and them old thin mouths all drawed in. . . ."

". . . and when they talk they whine through their noses. . . ."

". . . like starved cats!"

"And Lawd, they lazy's the day is long. . . ."

". . . laying around in the sun. . . ."

". . . like tired-out hounddogs. . . ."

". . . licking their sores. . . ."

". . . and about ready to die!"

"And *mean?*"

"I ain't never seen folks what could laugh at suffering like they can."

"When other folks is happy, they suffer. . . ."

". . . and when other folks is suffering, they's happy!"

"I think Gawd must've made them folks wrongsideoutward."

> *"Don't like a liver*
> *Don't like hash*
> *Rather be a nigger*
> *Than poor white trash. . . ."*

"Lawd, when I was down South I use' to dream about Chicago!"

"Chicago seemed like the Promised Land!"

> *"Heaven is up*
> *South is down*
> *Lawd, Lawd*
> *I'm Northward Bound. . . ."*

"I remember the day I left, the train was so full of black folks coming North I had to stand up all the way to Chicago."

"A white guy who was looking for men to work in the stockyards asked me if I wanted to come, and I walked off, just walked off and caught the train."

"When folks told me about the North I couldn't believe it was true."

"Yeah, a lot of the old folks said it was just a lie to trick us up North so's the white folks up here could put us in slavery."

"I remember little boys walking around singing: *'Lawd, I'd ruther be a lamppost in Chicago than the President of Miss'sippi. . . .'*"

"And there was another song: *'I'm going to shake the dust of the South off my feet forever. . . .'*"

"Them was the days when we lived in hope."

"Yeah, but there was some good times in the South. . . ."

". . . when the white folks wasn't nowhere around. . . ."

". . . and the guys all gathered around in the backyard with guitars. . . ."

". . . playing and singing. . . ."

". . . and that evening sun going down. . . ."

". . . red like blood. . . ."

". . . and that old lazy river flowing South. . . ."

". . . and the womenfolks standing around sort of sadlike. . . ."

". . . waiting for you to say something. . . ."

154

". . . and you feel like you want to

>*"Shake it to the East*
>*Shake it to the West*
>*Shake it to the one*
>*You love the best. . . ."*

". . . and you got a aching in your bones. . . ."
". . . like you got to do what you want to do or die!"
"Yeah, Gawd! That feeling that makes you want to howl and moan. . . ."
". . . like a wildcat in a swamp!"
"Lawd, today!"
"This life and another one!"
"There was some good days in the South. . . ."
"Yeah, in the summer. . . ."
". . . when you didn't have nothing to do but lay in the sun and live."
"I use' to get out of the bed feeling tired, didn't want to do *nothing!*"
"Look like the South just makes a man feel like a millionaire!"
"I use' to go swimming in the creek. . . ."
"Fishing's what I love! Seems like I can smell them catfish frying right now!"
"And in the summer when the Magnolia trees is in blossom. . . ."
". . . you can smell 'em for half a mile!"
"And them sunflowers. . . ."
". . . and honeysuckles."
"You know, we use' to break them honeysuckles off the stem and suck the sweetness out of 'em."
"And them plums. . . ."
". . . so ripe they was busting open!"
"And surgarcane. . . ."
". . . and blackberries. . . ."
". . . juicy and sweet!"
"And in the summer at night the sky's so full of stars you think they going to fall. . . ."
". . . and the air soft and warm. . . ."
". . . smelling like water."
"And them long rains in the winter. . . ."
". . . rain sometimes for a week. . . ."
". . . and you set inside and roast corn and sweet potatoes!"
"Boy, the South's good. . . ."
". . . and bad!"
"It's Heaven. . . ."
". . . and Hell. . . ."
". . . all rolled into one!"

"The only difference between the North and the South is, them guys down there'll kill you, and these up here'll let you starve to death."

"Well, I'd rather die slow than to die fast!"

"Jews, Catholics, and niggers. . . ."

". . . the South's sure hard on 'em!"

"But shucks, I don't mind how bad they treat them Jews. They run 'em out of the old countries and they come over here and treat us just like the folks over there treated them."

"Yeah, when a white man's hard on a Jew it's 'cause he's got it coming to 'im."

"And them Catholics. . . . Them's the sly guys!"

"Yeah, all that plotting with the Pope."

"I reckon the white folks is right when they's against them."

"But why in hell they so hard on us?"

"We don't do nothing."

"And we been in this country long's any of 'em."

"They say they lynch us to keep their women pure. . . ."

"Hell, I don't believe that!"

"You know, a friend of mine told me a story once. He was going down South with two Northern white men, driving the car for 'em. They got down in Miss'sippi and was riding along a country road when they spied three white gals, flagging 'em. . . . Well, the white guy told the black guy to stop the car. He did. The white gals got in and all of 'em started drinking. After awhile they felt like doing it, and so they went into the woods. Now this black guy was scared. The white men carried their gals off and started pumping away. But this black guy just stood up. The gal asked 'im what was the matter. He wouldn't even talk. He just stood there with his mouth open, thinking about all the black men the white folks done killed and burned. And this gal was laying there squirming and panting, hot as fire. She got so mad she pulled off her shoe and beat 'im over the head with it, run 'im back to the car. . . . That shows you there ain't no trouble with black men bothering white women. Hell, they scared. . . ."

"I know I was scared."

"Shucks, I wouldn't hardly look at one when I was down South."

"If a white woman had smiled at me I would've started running."

"I saw 'em hang a man once."

"Yeah?"

"He was a young guy who'd done killed a white man. . . ."

"Was he scared?"

156

"Naw, he just stood still with his eyes on the sky and didn't say a mumbling word. . . ."

"Lawd!"

"The old sheriff just pulled the handle and the trap door dropped and the man shot down and that rope got tight. . . . It was almost dark and he just hung there, jerking a little with his head to one side. Pretty soon he was dead."

"Gee, I ain't never seen no hanging."

"Me neither."

"Well, don't see none, 'cause you won't be able to sleep for a week."

"The white folks just done made up in their minds they ain't going to let no black man rise!"

"But the Bible says Ethiopia's going to stretch forth her hand some day."

"Look like old Mussellinni's done stopped that."

"Aw, that don't mean nothing. You can't tell what plan Gawd's got up His sleeve."

"Naw, you can't. Gawd wouldn't let nothing like that happen without doing *some*thing about it."

"He's going to fix 'em some day."

"It'll be like the preacher say: A Great GettingUp Morning!"

"Shucks, the preachers say we black folks was a great race once."

"Sure, them was the times when we was in Africa."

"Black folks ruled the world then."

"You see, every race gets it's chance. The black folks, then the yellow folks, then them Greeks, and on down the line. . . . The white folks is holding the fort now."

"But them white folks done covered up our records so's we won't know how great we is."

"They say there was a great black man in Roosia."

"Who?"

"His name was Pumpkin, wasn't it?"

"What he do?"

"He wrote books."

"That make 'im great?"

"Oh, yeah. I heard of 'im. I heard a preacher say he got killed fighting with a white man. . . ."

"Now, that sounds something like it."

"They say old Solomon was a black man."

"He was the wisest man in the world."

"Some folks say Peter was black."

"You ever see them pictures with black angels on 'em?"

"Sure."

"We got one at home."

157

"A colored guy done wrote a book proving that *Jesus* was black!

"He might've been. If he was, these white folks'd keep it from us so's we can't have no pride in ourselves."

"Aw, them white bastards is slick!"

"But things can't go on like this always."

"You know, I wish there was a man somewhere who knowed how to lead and who could lead . . ."

"A guy who wouldn't steal. . . ."

". . . and lie. . . ."

". . . and grab your woman when your back is turned."

". . . and who would know how to speak out all these things so folks'd understand 'em. . . ."

". . . and who wouldn't be scared!"

"There'll be a man like that some day. . . ."

". . . and things start to change then."

"You know, honest, for something like that I wouldn't mind maybe fighting and dying."

"Yeah, when you feel that a lot of folks feel like you feel."

"I reckon that's what the preacher calls faith."

"It's something you hate like hell to talk about, but you's always wishing somebody else felt that way, too."

"A lot of times I been wanting to do things I just wouldn't do."

"And I bet a lot of other folks feel the same way."

"Now. . . . Wait a minute. . . . Now, you see, if *all* the folks felt like that, why in hell don't they *do* something?"

"Do what?"

"What we's talking about. . . ."

"Aw, hell! Some guy's got something *you* want, and you got something *he* wants, and when you start to do something you bump into each other. . . ."

"Yeah, like you see trains crashing up in the movies."

"But, shucks, if we all was in the same train going in the same direction. . . ."

"Aw, man, ain't no sense in talking about things like this."

"Yeah, the more you talk about 'em the more you can't feel 'em."

"You know, the white folks who built this country must've felt something like that."

"Yeah, but they don't feel like that now. One half of 'em's mad at the other."

"Say you remember that colored guy who use' t' preach over the radio?"

"That guy who said everybody's got to come under one command?"

"Yeah."

"Maybe that's what he was talking about."

"Maybe it was."

"But it'd take a strong guy to make all these folks come under one command."

"You telling me?"

"Like old Hitler. . . ."

". . . and Mussellinni."

"Nigger, Wops, Frogs, Dagos, Chinks, Japs, Kikes . . . Lawd, it's a mess!"

> *"Red, white, and blue*
> *Your Pa's a lousy Jew*
> *Your Ma's a dirty Dago*
> *And what in hell is you? . . ."*

"Well, I reckon the best thing for a guy to do is get together with a woman."

"State Street Mama!"

> *"My name is Jim Taylor*
> *My john is a whaler*
> *And my balls weigh ninety-nine pound*
> *If you know any ladies*
> *Who want any babies*
> *Just tell 'em Jim Taylor's in town. . . ."*

"Hahaha!"

"Hohoho!"

"Say, you remember the first meat you ever had?"

"Gee, it makes me laugh to think about it!"

"Who was the first meat you ever had, Al?"

"Aw, I don't know."

"Naw, I don't want to tell that."

"You scared?"

"Naw."

"Tell us. . . ."

"Aw, she was my cousin. . . . Hahaha!"

"Hohoho!"

"Who was your first meat, Jake."

"Well, my Ma sent me out in the country to visit my uncle and he wasn't home. His wife asked me to stay all night. . . ."

"What happened?"

"Hell, you *know* what happened!"

"I bet you was like a wild bull!"

159

"Aw, naw, now! *She* started at me!"

"I *bet* she didn't!"

"And the next morning I run all the way home!"

"You, Slim? Come on. . . ."

"It was a preacher's wife. He was away preaching a funeral. . . ."

"Ain't that a bitch?"

"How old was you?"

"Just thirteen. . . ."

"Come on, now. You, Bob. . . ."

"All I got to say is, a young boy ain't got no conscience. . . . Hahaha!"

"You never forget that first time."

"A woman always wants you."

"Yeah, if you ain't got nothing else you can always get a woman."

"But some women's so damn much trouble."

"They always want so much."

"Just a handful of gimme. . . ."

". . . and a lifeful of sorrow!"

"You can't do with 'em and you can't do without 'em!"

"Gee, that reminds me!"

"What?"

"Ain't I showed you them pictures?"

"What pictures?"

"You ain't showed us nothing."

"Them pictures I bought from the Chink?"

"Naw!"

"Boy, this is the hottest stuff in town!"

"Let's see 'em!"

"Look and weep, niggers!"

"Read what it say!"

"Hold it up so I can see!"

"Wait a minute and let Jake read it!"

> *"I love you once*
> *I love you twice*
> *I love you next*
> *To Jesus Christ. . . ."*

"Open 'em up!"

"Yeah, let's seem 'em!"

"Take your time, nigger!"

"Good Gawd Almighty!"

"Let me see 'em!"

"Quit pulling!"

"Don't tear 'em, nigger!"

"Hold the thing up!"

"Boy, look how he's got her!"

"Look how he's holding her!"

"He's riding her like a stallion!"

"He's riding her like a bicycle!"

"And she look like she likes it!"

"Sure she likes it!"

"Look at her eyes!"

"And her stommick!"

"She's biting her lips!"

"Come on, man! Let's see the next one!"

"Wheeeeeeeeee!"

"Do, re, mi, fa, sol, la, ti, do!"

"If he ain't got a grip on her!"

"Hold 'em up and let me see 'em!"

"Look like she's about to scream!"

"Look at them tits!"

"Lawd, today!"

"Good Gordin Gin!"

"Get off my foot!"

"You act like you gone crazy."

"That's a different woman from what was in the others!"

"Yeah, but it's the same man."

"And she looks like a real young girl."

"Look like she's gone to sleep."

"You'd look that way too if you had in you what she's got in her."

"Turn it over. Let's see the next one."

"Hunh! Now, ain't that something!"

"How can folks do things like that?"

"Doggone it, that's going too far for me!"

"Folks'll do *any*thing."

"They must pay folks a lot of money to take their pictures that way."

"Nigger, put them pictures in your pocket."

"Where you get 'em from?"

"I bought 'em from a Chink."

"How much?"

"Five bucks."

"He got any more?"

"I don't know. You'll have to see 'im."

"You know, them pictures must've been made in France."

"The Chink said they was made in France. That's how come they cost so much."

"They say French folks is immoral."

"Yeah, that's where all the freakish stuff comes from."

"A French woman'll do *any*thing!"

"You ought to hear some of them soljers talk that went to France."

161

"Gee, I'd like to go to France."

"Me too."

"Me too."

"Me too."

"Man, you know one thing? A woman's *funny!*"

"Oh, they funny, all right."

"Ain't it queer how a man just keeps thinking about 'em?"

"Just can't seem to get 'em off your mind."

"There's something about 'em that just draws you, no matter what."

"And you can't help yourself."

"And that feeling a woman gives you!"

"Jeeesus!"

"Boy, it's a terrible thing!"

"It's like fire!"

"Like ice!"

"Like a 'lectric shock!"

"It knocks you out!"

"It gets you all over. . . ."

". . . in your head. . . ."

". . . and legs. . . ."

". . . and thighs. . . ."

". . . like somebody pouring warm water over you!"

"It lifts you up and then lets you down. . . ."

". . . and you want to go to sleep. . . ."

". . . but in a little while you want to go again."

"It's a funny feeling."

"It's the greatest feeling in the world."

"Yeah, but a man couldn't stand that feeling for long."

"Naw, he just couldn't bear it."

"It'd kill 'im."

Part Three:

RATS' ALLEY

. . . But at my back in a cold blast I hear
The rattle of the bones, and chuckle spread from ear to ear.

—T. S. Eliot's *Wasteland*

. . . A shot, a scream, a cloud of smoke—all in a split second of time. The bullet entered the left side of President Lincoln's head, passed through the brain, and stopped just short of the left eye. He was rushed to a room opposite Ford's Theatre, and there he lingered among tender friends until morning. At twenty-two minutes past seven o'clock he died. As he breathed his last, Secretary Stanton said:

"Now, he belongs to the ages. . . ."

I.

When they were least expecting it, when their minds had strayed on a daydreaming pilgrimage, the gong for quitting time boomed throughout the Mailing Division.

"TWELVE-THIRTY CLERKS CHECKOUT!"

As though they were dead men suddenly come to life, they dropped the mail and ran to the timecard racks; then, holding to banisters, they galloped down the winding steel stairs three steps at a time and pushed their way into the smelly washroom.

"Make it snappy!" called Jake, rubbing white lather about his neck.

"Cccome on, fffor Cchrissake!" coughed Slim. "I wwwant to wwwash!"

"Move over!" said Al.

"Youall wait for me!" Bob yelled, running for the commodes.

As they received their hats, coats, and canes their faces assumed expressions of healthy interest. Legs and arms which had moved listlessly swung with buoyant energy; voices which had been low monotones rose in relieved shouts.

"Let's go!" called Jake, jamming his arms awkwardly into his coat.

"Coming!"

They filed out upon the front steps and stood huddled amid swirling snowflakes with their coat collars turned up. Heavy spouts of vapor rolled from their lips and lingered a moment in the cold air, then vanished. About them the muffled thunder of traffic crashed in a falling shroud of white. The headlights of autos swerved around corners and glared momentarily.

"Well where do we go from here?" asked Al.

"How about some cigars?" asked Jake.

"Sure thing."

A few minutes later they were standing in a doorway, puffing cigars and looking at the passing traffic with a superb detachment. They were almost satisfied now, but not quite. Each felt that something was lacking, and that lack hungered over and above ordinary hunger; they could feel it in their stomachs, in their legs, even in the tips of their fingers. Jake rolled his cigar from one corner of his mouth to the other.

"Say, how about some likker?"

"Now you talking!"

With a halfpint flask sagging in each of his coat pockets, Jake stood again in a doorway.

"It's near eleven bells," said Al.

"Let's get going."

"I want to buy a paper first," said Slim. "Here, boy!"

"Wheeeee!" Al whistled through his teeth for a roving taxi.

Brakes screamed; a car swerved to the curb; a door swung open, and the four of them piled in.

"Forty-five fifty-eight Calumet!" Jake called.

"O.K."

As the car lumbered southward over snow-covered streets, Jake nestled into a corner and felt the flasks pressing against his sides.

"How about a little nip?"

Jake, Al, and Slim drank.

"Aw, come on, Bob. One shot won't hurt you."

"Naw."

"Aw, man, take a drink."

Bob sat tensely on the edge of the seat. His lips moved several times, but he said nothing. Jake pushed the bottle into his hands; he held it, his lips parted in fascination and indecision.

"Don't be a wet blanket!"

Bob tilted the flask and drank.

"It sure can't kill me," he said, blowing to cool the fiery burn.

"You don't live but once," said Al.

Slim pulled out the newspaper and squinted at the headline.

"What's the news?" asked Jake, closing his eyes.

"They say Japan's done grabbed *all* Manchooria."

"Yeah?"

"And they say a hundred million Chinks in China's done gone Red."

"Now them Chinks is funny folks," said Bob.

"Yeah, they eat with sticks."

"They eat rats, too."

"And rotten eggs."

"A Chink'll do *any*thing."

"They say they killing up more Jews in Germany," read Slim.

"*Some*body always killing them Jews!"

"You know, I saw in the papers where they plotting to rule the whole world."

"Yeah, they got all the gold hid away now."

"Them rookies is *slick*."

166

"And they done lynched another nigger down South," said Slim.

"Yeah?" asked Jake, turning slightly.

"They burnt 'im alive," said Slim.

"Well, Gawddammit, they ought to lynch 'em if they ain't got no better senses to stay down there."

"I wouldn't live in a place like that," said Al.

"That's how come I left," said Bob.

"They say old Roosia's done gone and got a army of eighteen million men," said Slim.

"Aw, them Reds can't fight," said Al.

"And here's the picture of a guy what can play the violin with his toes," said Slim.

"With his *toes*?"

"Let's see it!"

"Gee, that's going some!"

"Say, I seen a guy shoot pool blindfolded once."

"I seen a guy play a guitar standing on his *head*."

"Some folks can do almost anything."

"It's a natural born gift."

Slim threw the paper aside and they rode awhile in silence. Jake thought of the one hundred dollars on his hip and sang:

"Yellow taxis, yellow money, yellow women. . . ."

They chuckled and puffed languidly. Now and then they took the black weeds out of their mouths and eyed the glowing tips.

"Damn good smoke."

"You bet."

"Draws well."

"Yeah."

The taxi swung to a snowbanked curb.

"Well, here we is, boys!" Jake announced. The snow had slackened a bit. As Jake paid the bill Slim led the way into the vestibule.

"Looks like a swell joint."

"Hope they got some red-hot mamas up there."

"Don't worry about that."

In answer to Slim's three pressures of the bell the door buzzed. Midway up the steps they could hear the sound of muffled music and the rhythm of pounding feet. At the top of the landing they were met by a buxom, brown-skinned woman.

"Hello, Rose!" called Jake.

"Glory be! If it ain't my four Aggravating Papas!" said Rose, flinging her arms wide.

167

"And you don't know how aggravating," said Jake as he caught her around the waist.

"Look like you's ready for business tonight," said Rose.

"You'll be surprised," said Slim, slapping her fleshy buttocks.

Rose shook her finger at them playfully.

"Come on, now! Be a good boy for mama! I'm mighty proud you brought your pals along, Jake. We can have some good times here. . . . Now, youall just come right in and take off your coats and hats and hang 'em in the closet and make yourselves at home. What you don't see, ask for it. And when you gets hungry step back in the diningroom and eat some of the best chitterlings you ever tasted. Ain't no need for youall to be a bit bashful around here. Just throw your troubles away. . . ."

They pushed into a big room jammed with dancers. Shouts, laughter, and snatches of song swung through the smoky air. A threepiece jazz band—a cornet, a drum, and a piano—made raucous music in a corner. There were gamblers, pimps, petty thieves, dope peddlers, smallfry politicians, grafters, racketeers of various shades, athletes, high school and college students in search of "life", and hordes of sex-eager youngsters. The women were white, ivory, yellow, light brown, medium brown, solid brown, dark brown, near black, and black. They wore red, yellow, brown, blue, purple, and black gowns with V shapes reaching down almost to their waists. Their bosoms were high and bulging, and they danced with an obvious exaggeration of motion.

With the stump of his cigar clamped in his teeth, Jake stood just inside the door and looked over the crowd. He watched the women's bodies swing and a warm glow spread from his stomach to his chest. A deep sense of ease and freedom pervaded him; he stood with his legs wide apart and with his thumbs hooked in the armholes of his vest. *This don't look like a bad crowd.* He knew some of them from other times. There was Blue Juice, a pimp who boasted that he controlled more women than any single Negro on the South Side. There was Ben Kitty, known far and wide for his skill at billiards. And there was a tall, slender, brown-skinned man called One Barrel; it was reputed that he was so stingy he breathed only out of one barrel of his nose. *Naw, this ain't bad at all.* Jake smiled and listened to voices call to and fro.

"Have a sip, Daddy!"

"Come on and let's get lowdown!"

"I don't care! I don't care!"

"Whip that piano, Bopeep!"

"Aw, dance that thing!"

"Lawd! Lawd!"

Bob tugged at Jake's sleeve.

"Say, Jake?"

"Yeah?"

"Slip me something. I'm going to shoot some craps in the backroom."

"Sure," said Jake, laughing and slipping a five dollar bill into Bob's hand. "You just out of luck, Bob."

"Call me when youall's ready to eat."

"O.K."

Slim grabbed a stocky, mulatto girl and started dancing. Al was talking to a thin black girl.

"Say, partner?"

Jake turned and faced a short, skinny, black man with bloodshot eyes.

"Want some weeds?"

"Naw."

"Only twobits."

"Naw."

"Aw, come on."

"Naw, I tell you!"

Jake walked off. He did not want to smoke any Marijuana cigarettes. *Likker's good enough for me.* He saw some of the younger men and women huddled in corners sucking hungrily at cigarettes. They inhaled deeply, held the smoke in their lungs as long as they could, and beat their chests to absorb the essence of the smoke. *That's a sissy's way to get high.*

Jake lolled, his eyes roving somberly. He was trying to pick out a woman. Finally, he went to a yellow one who was walking alone to and fro in front of a window at the far end of the room. She was of medium height with broad hips and she welcomed him with a wide, wet smile. He walked her to the center of the floor and they swung into a dance.

"Where you been all my life?" he asked, tightening his arm.

"Where you been all *my* life?" she countered, nestling close.

Back and across the room they swayed like trees bending in strong winds. Feet went thrumpthrump, thrumpthrump, thrumpthrump. . . .

"Shake that thing!" somebody yelled.

"What's your name?" Jake asked his girl.

"Blanche, Sweet Papa. What might be yours?"

"Just Jake," he said, swinging her through a narrow opening between the dancers.

"You works in the Post Office, Sweet?"

"Sure thing, Baby."

169

"Look like you and me's going to hit it off O.K.," she said, throwing the naked part of her arm about his neck.

"I knows we is," he said.

"Sweet Papa," she breathed into his ear.

"How long you been in this joint?" he asked.

"About a week."

"Like it?"

"I don't mind."

"How's tricks."

"Slow."

"Don't look like a babe like you ought to have no trouble."

"Honey, these niggers ain't got no money."

"I got money."

"You look like it."

"Been in Chi long?"

"About a week, I told you."

"Oh, so you started right in here."

"Yeah, but I'm looking for a steady daddy."

"String along with me, Babe."

She laughed. They stood still in a tight knot of dancers and moved only their hips and knees. Jake looked at the yellow sweep of her bosom. *She ain't bad.* The music sank low, sobbing the *St. Louis Blues;* he felt Blanche rolling her stomach to him, softly. Their eyes met and his lips parted.

"Say?" he asked.

"What's the matter, Papa?"

"Who learned you that?"

"You'd be surprised."

Jake laughed and whirled her over the floor. *Naw, she ain't bad at all.*

"I'm hungry."

"Plenty of grub in the back."

"What you say, let's eat?"

"Just's you say, Papa."

Jake gathered his party and led them through two rear rooms and into a little curtained nook. Rose hovered above them.

"I had this table all saved just 'specially for youall," she said. "I thought youall'd want it sort of privatelike."

"You knows your stuff, Rose," said Jake.

"Nothing different," she answered.

"This is a mellow joint," said Al.

"How come you ain't got a gal?" Rose asked Bob.

"Oh, I'm laying off for awhile," Bob mumbled.

"He's teething," said Jake.

They laughed. Bob rolled his eyes, took out his flask, and swallowed a deep drink. Rose placed her hand tenderly on the back of his neck.

170

"Listen," she said. "When you gets well come and see me and I'll fix it so's you won't never have to teethe no more."

"I'll be around," said Bob.

"Now, youall get ready to eat a heap tonight," coaxed Rose, polishing the top of the table with her dishtowel.

"What you got that's good?" asked Jake.

"Well, I got some chitterlings, turnip greens cooked with smoked ribs, Spanish rice, slaw, spaghetti, egg cornbread, pigtails, barbecue, beer, and whiskey," sang Rose.

Al sucked back loose saliva.

"Hush your mouth!"

"Folks, order anything you want!" said Jake, with a sweeping wave of his hand.

"I wants some chitterlings," said Blanche.

"I wants some of that barbecue," said Slim's girl.

"Make it four chitterlings and four barbecues and beer and slaw all around," bawled Jake. "The stuff's on me tonight!"

"Coming up!" sang Rose.

"Have some cigarettes," said Jake.

They lit up and blew smoke into one another's faces. The men appraised the girls' lips, throats, shoulders, and bosoms. The girls sighed and looked wistfully at their plates.

"It's been a long time since we's been around with any Post Office dudes," sighed Blanche.

"Well, you got a good chance to make up for lost time tonight," said Jake.

There was a short silence during which each man edged his chair closer to the table.

The girls' eyes assumed lights of coy innocence and the men's jaws assumed lines of aggressiveness.

"Youall sure ought to see our rooms upstairs," suggested Blanche.

"Yeah?"

"We got the cutest beds. . . ."

"You know who we is?" asked Slim.

"Who?"

"We's the official bed inspectors," he said.

They laughed. The lights were lowered just enough to give the room a dreamlike air. The naked flesh of the women's arms gleamed satinly under the soft sheens of the floor lamp. Rose brought two long platters of steaming food.

"Go to it, folks! This ain't no dicty joint and you can eat till you bust!"

Rose went from glass to glass and poured foaming beer.

"I'm going to turn on the radio so's youall can have some music," she said as she left. "And if you want anything, just call."

"O.K."

171

A crashing chord of martial music rose and died away; a voice spoke.

> . . . At Antietam McClellan and Lee clashed in a sanguinary struggle in which the blood of twenty-two thousand men stained the soil. . . .

"What in hell is *that?*"

"Aw," drawled Bob, nodding sleepily. "That's that Civil War. . . ."

"Slide the salt down this way!"

"Give me that cornbread!"

"Hand me that sauce!"

"Llllet mmmme ssse. . . . Let me see that ssssslaw," coughed Slim.

The hot, greasy food was washed down by huge draughts of cold beer.

"More beer here, Rose!" Jake bawled.

"Coming, Mister Post Office Man!" she sang, sidling up to get the empty bottles.

They ate, ramming knives deep into their mouths.

"Pheeeeeeeeeeeeew!" exclaimed Al's girl. "I ain't going to eat no more. I'm scared of getting too fat."

"Too *fat?*"

"Yeah."

Al raised his eyes and looked intently at her fleshy bosom.

"Don't let a little thing like that worry you none, Sweetheart," he said eagerly through a mouthful of chitterlings whose grease oozed from the corners of his lips. "The fatter the berry the sweeter the juice!"

"Why, you naaaaaaasty maaaaaaan!" she said, widening her eyes in mock shame.

The girls dropped their knives and forks and covered their mouths with their hands to smother giggles. Jake, Al, and Bob, and Slim leaned back in chairs, opened their mouths as wide as their jaws would permit, clapped their hands protectingly over their swollen stomachs, and gave vent to a roar of merriment that drowned out the radio. When their guffaws had simmered down to mere sniffles, Jake asked Al:

"How you know about how much juice in a fat berry?"

"Oh, I know, all right," said Al, wiping the crumbs and grease from his lips with the back of his hand.

"Talk like you done had some business with fat berries," said Blanche.

"I ain't missed it," said Al.

They laughed again.

"If that's the case, you gals better eat a heap," said Slim.

"Oh, I reckon we got juice enough," said Blanche.

172

"You *sure?*" asked Jake.

"We *ought* to know," said Blanche.

"Who told you?" asked Jake.

"Ain't nobody never kicked on us none," said Blanche.

"That's fair enough," said Al, waving his fork. "If ain't nobody else kicked, then we can't kick."

"If our customers ain't satisfied, they tell us. If they is they tell others," said Blanche.

The four men bent low over their plates as their mouths flew open again. The girls clapped them heartily on their backs to increase their ribaldry.

> Now Sherman's troops were sweeping a belt many miles wide with the zest of men out for a holiday. They were robbing it of every edible thing. They burnt mills. They tore up railroads and piled the rails in blazing heaps and twisted them while still hot around the trunks of forest trees. . . .

"How's we doing!"

"Hey, hey!"

"Youall's O.K.," said Slim.

"You got my vote," said Al.

"Say, Rose! More chitterlings and barbacue here!" called Jake.

When they had sopped their plates and drained the last of the beer, they leaned back in their chairs, sighing and suppressing belches. The beer and hot food made them sleepy. Blanche yawned.

"Shucks, I feel like a snake what's done swallowed a chicken," she mumbled.

The men tried to smile, but could not; they were full and listless.

"Let's dance, folks," said Jake in a dead tone.

"O.K. with me," sighed Al.

No one moved. The music in the front room was now going so loud that they heard it even through the partitions. Feet went thrumpthrump, thrumpthrump, thrumpthrump. . . . The house seemed to rock in a vast darkness. The monotonous rhythm was like a thousand fingers tapping the taut skin of a kettle drum in the midst of a deep forest. At intervals the muffled cry of the cornet rose up and died away like the midnight wail of a lovesick tomcat. The piano moaned like a woman in labor.

"Aw, I want to dance," said Al's girl.

"Me too," said Slim's girl.

"O.K.," said Al.

No one moved. Jake yawned and belched.

"Rose!" he called.

"Coming!"

"How about some likker!"

"Sure thing!"

It was not until they had had four rounds of whiskey that they felt like moving.

"This stuff's really good," said Jake.

> . . . With malice toward none, with charity for all, with firmness in the right as God gives us to see the right, let us finish the work we are in. . . .

"Come on! Let's finish the bottle!"

"Yeah, let's drink!"

Bob swayed forward, slobbering.

"Yeeeeeeah, what to hell!"

II.

When the bottle was empty, Jake reached for his pocketbook, placed it upon the table, and exposed to view a thick wad of green bills. Blanche peeped into it and exclaimed:

"Lawd, man! You sure well-heeled!"

He smiled at her.

"What's the matter, Honey?" He turned to Rose. "What I owe you, Sweetmeat?"

"Just twelve fifty," she said diffidently.

Jake gave her three five dollar bills.

"Keep the change, Toots!"

"That's what I love about a sport!" sang Rose.

He led his party back to the front room. Stimulated by alcohol, they glided on to the floor in answer to the call of the music. Their limp bodies swayed bonelessly to every tug of the rhythm. The air was heavy and damp. They tightened their arms as the music grew personal, selfish, sexual. Their eyes became vague and dreamy. Stomach rubbed stomach. Sweat beaded on black temples. Nostrils gleamed. Thick lips grew wet and sagged, trembling when bodies were swung. Now and then a slight moan was heard; it was as though someone had become so charged with emotion that he could contain it no longer. The pounding piano, the incessant shuffling of feet, and the sobbing cornet invoked a spirit of emotional surrender so intense that its driving force manifested itself in the hard, drawn lines of their faces. Feet went thrumpthrump, thrumpthrump, thrumpthrump. . . . Rose

174

pushed her way into the center of the room and yelled:
"Is everybody happy?"

"In Heaven with my feets hanging out!"

"We's got the world in a jug. . . ."

". . . and the stopper in our hands!"

Rose filled her lungs and yelled again:

"I SAY, IS EVERYBODY HAPPY?"

"Yeah, Lawd!"

"WELL, GIVE 'EM SOME MUSIC AND LET 'EM DANCE THE TIME DOWN!"

The band beat out *Tiger Rag*. As Jake danced his head was tilted backward. The expression upon his face was peculiar, paradoxical; it was relaxed and flabby, yet somehow eager and watchful. There was in it a sort of childish trustfulness. The music caroled its promise of an unattainable satisfaction and lured him to a land whose boundaries receded with each step he took. When the music slowed he felt tired, but when it went faster, he went faster. Each time it reached a high pitch of intensity he verged on the limits of physical feeling, as though beyond this was nothing but sleep, death; but when it sank, quavering, sighing, disillusioned, his muscles slackened, hungering for more. The room became so crowded he could hardly move. Bopeep played *Is It True What They Say About Dixie?*, and he slid over the floor, shifting from foot to foot. With each twist of his shoulders he felt the yielding softness of Blanche's body; he placed the open palm of his right hand in the center of her back and pressed her closer to him; he straightened till he felt her touching him at almost every point; then he pranced and swayed in one spot in a tight knot of dancers, his lips hanging loose. Blanche's breath came warm on the side of his neck and he heard her whisper:

"That's murder, Papa."

"I want to be electrocuted," he said.

"Oh, play it, Mister Piano Man, play it!" a young, black girl yelled, breaking suddenly from her partner and dancing alone in the center of the room, flinging her legs and arms in all directions. The rest paused, formed a circle about her and began to clap their hands, each clap falling midway between the beats of the music and creating a sharp and imperious syncopation. The girl's eyes rolled wildly; her head bobbed back and forth and she flung her limbs heavily as though she were drugged with warm wine. She advanced with the palms of her hands holding hard to her thighs and retreated with the tips of her fingers pressed deep into the soft flesh of her stomach. The dance became slower and slower till nothing moved but the muscles in her hips. Finally she gaped her mouth like a fish out of water and sank to her knees, moaning:

175

"Lawd . . . Lawd. . . ."

"Do it, gal!"

"Show 'em you ain't scared!"

"Come on, Papa," Blanche urged. "Let's get in close where we can see."

"O.K., Baby."

He caught her around the waist and rammed his way into the crowd. All about him he felt the pressure of eager bodies. Blanche lunged suddenly and her arms clung to his neck for support. He held her on her feet.

"What's the matter?"

Blanche turned and sneered:

"Watch where you going, nigger!"

Jake whirled, ready for fight. A tall, black man bowed and grinned.

" 'Scuse me," he said meekly.

"How come you can't look where you walking?" Jake growled, starting forward.

Blanche pulled him back.

"Aw, Daddy, forget 'im. He ain't nobody."

Jake's jaws clamped tight and his eyes followed the man till he disappeared through a rear door. He felt good tonight; he felt like hitting somebody. *What he doing trying to run over me?*

Another girl had come into the center of the ring and was dancing to the tune of *Sister Kate.* Her hair flew about her head, sometimes screening her face. Her thin body whirled like a spinning top; her dress rose and floated at the level of her hips, revealing the smooth, cool brown of her legs.

"Dance that thing, gal!" croaked a man who was so drunk he looked cross-eyed.

Another girl came in. Bopeep played *Handy Man.* With her feet still, she swayed her hips and crooned:

> *"He hauls my ashes*
> *He strokes my fiddle*
> *Threads my needle*
> *Creams my wheat*
> *Lawd, he's a damn good man to have around. . . ."*

"Do it, Sadie, do it!"

Jake felt giddy; he clapped his hands, closed his eyes, threw back his head, and yelled:

"DO IT A LONG OLD TIME!"

A stout, black woman waddled into the center of the ring and called to Bopeep:

"Play my piece!"

She sang in a cracked, nasal alto, uttering one line while she walled her eyes to the left, and uttering another line while she walled her eyes to the right.

> *"Two old maids in a folding bed*
> *One turned to the other, and said:*
> *'Yes, we have no bananas, Delight,*
> *We have no bananas tonight. . . .' "*

Jake bent double with laughter.

> *"Two old maids in a folding bed*
> *One turned to the other and said:*
> *'Darling, you are growing old;*
> *There're silver threads among your gold. . . .' "*

Jake hugged Blanche and screamed. When the song ended she danced. Her flaccid buttocks and bosom shivered like fluid. Her eyes were closed, her face lifted ceilingward, her lips tightly compressed. She seemed absorbed in an intense feeling burning in her stomach and she clawed her fingers hungrily in the air.

"Pick them cherries, gal! Pick 'em!"

Abruptly, the dance changed; her legs leaped into the air; her body ran riot with a goal of its own. The muscles of her stomach rose and fell insatiably. The music whirled faster and she whirled faster. She seemed to have lost all conscious control, seemed possessed by the impelling excitement of her nervous system. The climax came when she clasped her knees together in a steellike clamp and wrapped her arms tightly about her heaving bosom. She trembled from head to feet, her face distorted in orgiastic agony.

A thin black woman grabbed her boy friend and bit his ear till blood came.

"Lawd, today!"

Jake pulled Blanche into a corner. His eyes burned red and he bit his lips.

"Say, how about it?" he asked tensely, huskily.

"About what?"

"What you going to charge?"

He held her arm in a nervous grip.

"Quit! You hurting my arm!"

"Aw, come on."

She disengaged herself and cooed:

"What you talking about, Honey?"

"I want you. Ain't that plain? Now, what you going to charge me?"

Blanche smiled and walked off as though she had not heard. He followed, like a little dog.

177

"Aw, come on!"

"Not much," she said, looking off.

"But *how* much?"

"I'll charge you what it's worth."

"What's it worth?"

"Well. . . ."

"Well, *what?*"

She walked off again. Jake tagged her sleeve. She turned and looked at him intently.

"How much you got, Big Boy?"

"What's that got to do with it?"

She rounded her lips and spoke coolly:

"Ten dollars."

"Jeeesus," said Jake. "What you think I is?"

"Take it or leave it, Big Boy. If you don't want to do business, I'm moving on. . . ."

"Wait a minute."

He frowned, dropped his cigarette, crushed it with his heel, and blew out a lungful of smoke. *Ten bucks is a lot of money. But, shucks. . . .*

"Where can we go?"

"Upstairs."

"O.K.," he said. "What about my pals, two more?"

"Stay here. I'll see if I can't make it ten apiece."

Impatiently, he waited in a corner with his hands jammed into his pockets. He saw Blanche talking with Blue Juice at the far end of the room. Blue Juice was looking at him, and the shadow of a doubt flitted across his roused senses. He lit another cigarette, still watching Blanche. *What. . . . What she talking to him. . . .* He looked away. A relaxation was settling in his nerves. *I'm going to buy some more likker,* he thought as he clinked the coins in his pocket. Blanche came back smiling.

"It's O.K.," she said.

"Come on," said Jake. "Let's see Rose. I want some likker."

When in the back room he took the bottle from Rose and reached for his pocketbook. It was not in his hip pocket. He felt the others, then sat the bottle down and went through each pocket, his lips hanging open.

"Where's my money?" he mumbled.

"Is you done lost something, Sugar?" Blanche asked.

"I can't find my money."

He searched his pockets again, took a step backward and looked from Blanche to Rose.

"Somebody done got my money," he said incredulously.

"Maybe you dropped it somewhere," suggested Rose.

Jake headed for the rear room where they had eaten. Rose and Blanche followed, looking at each other. He jerked back the chairs, looked under the table. It was not there. He stood silently and stared at the floor.

"Is you done lost it, Honey?" asked Blanche, tearful with distress.

Jake looked at her and his mind cleared slowly. *I done been tricked!* But by whom? How? Then he remembered the tall, black Negro who had bumped into him. He remembered Blanche clinging to his neck, diverting his attention from the man

"Did that black nigger what bumped into me take my money?"

"What you talking about Sweetheart?"

"You know what I'm talking about!"

"I swear I don't!"

"That nigger what bumped into me when we was watching 'em dancing!"

"What nigger?" pleaded Blanche.

"That sonofabitch!"

Jake whirled and elbowed his way through the crowd. Rose and Blanche trailed. He stood in the center of the front room and stared at the dancers. The man was nowhere around. He turned to Blanche.

"Where's the nigger?" he growled.

"You mean the man I cussed at?"

"You know Gawddamn well what I mean?"

"Honey, that man been gone from here."

"Where he gone?"

"How I know?"

"What kind of a looking man was he?" asked Rose, tenderly placing her hand on his sleeve. Jake opened his mouth to answer, but no words came. He felt like a fool. He wanted to grab something and smash it. Grab just anything and smash it to death. He knew it was useless to try to get his money now, and knowing filled him with rage. *These lowlife bastards! I ain't going to let 'em play me cheap and get away with it! Ain't no man alive going to play me for a sucker!* The room grew misty and he looked at Blanche, at her yellow throat, at her red lips, at her wide, dark eyes.

"I don't want no trouble," he drawled.

"Oh, Lawd!" moaned Rose, wringing her hands. "Mister Jake, we ain't got your money."

Jake felt people crowding around him and he gave a hard shove with his elbow.

"Don't crowd me now," he said huskily. " 'Cause I might hurt somebody."

They backed away and left him standing in an empty

179

circle. He could not take his eyes off Blanche's yellow face. His muscles were flexing slowly.

"I'm asking you for the last time to tell me who got my money," he said.

"That man's gone, Honey," whined Blanche.

He grabbed her arm.

"Where he go!"

"Turn me loose! You crazy!"

Jake raised his palm.

"You know who got my money!"

"Don't you hit me!" she screamed.

Jake grabbed for her and felt a hard hand on his shoulder. He was spun around.

"Don't you touch that woman!"

He looked into the black face of Blue Juice.

"Hunh?" Jake asked

"I don't chew my tobacco but once," spat Blue Juice.

He saw Ben Kitty and One Barrel standing ready for him, their legs wide apart, their hands thrust deep into their pockets. His neck flushed hot as fire. He had been robbed and these men were here to see that he did not bother Blanche who had helped to rob him. He swallowed and something seemed to turn upsidedown in his stomach. *They got my money. These bastards!*

"Where's the nigger that bumped into me?"

"Go find 'im!" said Blue Juice.

"I'd like to make you tell where he is!" Jake said to Blanche.

"Do it," said Blue Juice. "Do it and get your gutstring cut loose."

Jake saw Bob, Al, and Slim edge into the crowd.

"What's the matter, Jake."

"Somebody bothering you?"

"Say, what's this?"

"These bastards done rolled me," said Jake, emboldened by the presence of his friends.

"You calling me a bastard?" asked Blue Juice, stepping closer.

The crowd closed in and Jake felt himself being pushed against a wall. The music had stopped and he could hear his blood beating in his temples. His breath came fast and short.

"The nigger who took my dough's a bastard!" he said stubbornly.

"Did I take your dough?" asked Blue Juice.

Jake did not answer.

"Just say I did and I'll make you think you's a cat trying to cover up mess on a tin roof!"

"Who got your money, Jake?" asked Al.

"This woman here knows who got it," said Jake.

"She don't know," said Blue Juice.

"What you taking up for her, for?" asked Jake.

" 'Cause I'm man enough to," said Blue Juice.

"It ain't no skin off your nose if I make that bitch tell!"

"Don't you call her a bitch!"

"I *did*!" said Jake with hot pride.

He saw the blow coming and tried to duck, but tried too late. It caught him low on the neck; a pain shot through his chest; the room tilted and he fell flat on his face. He heard screams, heard Al and Slim calling. He scrambled to his feet and reached for Blue Juice. Something hit him at the base of the skull and the world went red, then grey. He was on the floor, in a world of grey pain, hearing screams and pounding feet. His whole life flowed hotly into his eyes, his stomach, his hands. *I'll kill 'im! I'll kill 'im!* He rolled over and tried to get up; he was still on his knees when something cold touched his temple, like cold metal it was, and it touched lightly, like a feather. He felt himself pitching forward, felt his fingers clawing weakly at the ridges in the wooden floor, and then suddenly the world went black. . . .

III.

Jake Jake Jake. His head sagged from side to side. *Jake Jake Jake.* He heard someone calling. *Hunh? Hunh?* He was trying to answer, trying to see where he was, wondering what made everything so awfully cold. A hard pain throbbed in his temples and at the base of his skull. A white and black world wavered before his eyes, then slowly righted itself, grew real, solid, freezing. His strength came gradually and his feet slipped on ice as he tried to stand.

"Jake! Jake!"

"Yeeeeeah," he drawled.

"How you feel? You O.K.?"

"Yeah."

He raised his eyes and saw Slim bending over and coughing out great white plumes of vapor. Bob was lurching near a fence, moaning. He understood now. They were in an alley. The snow had stopped and the sky had cleared to a hazy blue. An icy wind ached his face and burned the tips of his ears. He wanted to sink into the ground and sleep forever.

"Come on," said Al. "Let's go somewhere and get warm."

They struggled to the street and stumbled into a beer tavern. Jake flopped limply into a chair, propped his elbows on a table, held his head in his hands, and closed his eyes. *Gawddamn everything!*

"If I had a gun I'd go back up there and blow that whore's brains out," he groaned.

"Aw, forget her. Them guys'd kill you," said Al.

"That's a nest of rattlesnakes," said Slim.

"Every nigger in that joint had a gun or a knife or a blackjack."

"I kept feeling that whore was tricking me," Jake mumbled.

Bob lay with his head cradled in his arms.

"Wake up Bob!" said Al.

"What's the matter with 'im?" asked Jake.

"He's almost out. His dose and that whiskey just about fixed 'im."

Jake sorted out some coins.

"Here, get a halfpint," he said, giving the money to Al.

The three of them drank. They tried to awaken Bob, but he would not move.

"Somebody'll have to lug 'im home," sighed Jake.

"Slim and me'll take 'im," said Al. "We live his way."

"Lawd, but what happened? The last thing I remember I was trying to get a piece of that Blue Juice."

"They ganged you."

"Them guys is in a syndicate."

"We had to battle like wildcats to get you out of there alive."

"Old Ben Kitty was on you like white on rice."

"The whole mob of 'em was trying to do you in."

"It was old One Barrel what socked you behind the head, then I grabbed 'im."

"And old Blue Juice hit you in the temple with brass knuckles."

"Yeah," said Jake. "I thought the whole building had done fell on me. They hurt youall?"

"Naw, they backed up a little when they saw we'd fight."

"But boy, if it hadn't been for Rose pleading and screaming they was planning on using guns."

"And that Blanche dame did a quick fadeout."

"I saw her with a knife a foot long."

"That bitch!" said Jake.

"Where in Gawd's name you find that place?" asked Slim.

"Some bird down at the *Nook* told me to go there."

"He sure sent you into a mess of trouble."

"Some guy wanted to call the Law and Rose almost scratched his eyes out."

"I'm sure glad didn't no Law come."

"Yeah, they'd've been hard on us at the job about getting in jail."

"It would've been the end of me," sighed Jake.

Al clenched his fist and let it fall disgustedly.

"Just when we had them dames all lined up, this had to happen!"

"Jeeesus, look at me!" Jake demanded, almost indignantly. "Every red cent of that hundred dollars is gone. I'm right where I started!"

"Aw, hell! Ain't no use in thinking about it."

"Naw, you'll go nuts then."

They drank again.

"My head feels big's a barrel."

"What time you got?"

"Three-thirty."

"Jeeesus!"

"Is it that late?"

"Yep."

"Let's get going."

"Yeah, we got to work tomorrow."

But they did not move. Above their heads an old clock ticked away the time. Jake blew his nose, pulled the stopper out of the bottle, drank and passed it around.

"Come on, let's get some sleep."

Al and Slim lifted Bob. Jake walked alone, rocking a little and pushing his flask into his hip pocket. He caught his breath as he went through the door; the wind was keen and painful.

"It's cold!"

"It must be below zero!"

As they huddled in the doorway, Bob lurched toward the ground. Al caught him.

"Try to stand up, Bob! You ain't no baby!"

They lit cigarettes behind turned up coat collars.

"I sure would've been in a tough spot if it hadn't been for youall," sighed Jake.

"We got to watch out sharp next time."

"Yeah, we got to be careful."

Jake yawned.

"I'm sleepy."

"Me too."

"Let's get out of this cold."

They stepped gingerly to the sidewalk.

"Well," sighed Al. "I'll do you like the farmer did the potato."

"Plant you now and dig you later."

Slim laughed without opening his mouth.

"Aw, we had a good time, anyway."

"Oh, yeah."

"Sure."

Slim shifted restlessly from foot to foot and looked around.

"Say, how about another drink?" he asked abruptly.

"Sure," said Jake.

They drank again and licked their lips. Bob began to whimper.

"It's coming down on 'im again," said Al.

Bob broke from Al and crawled on his hands and knees in the snow. When Al tried to lift him, he fought him off and beat his fists against the air.

"He's wet," said Al.

"Pick 'im up," said Jake. "Don't let 'im wallow in that snow."

Bob bent his head to his knees and screamed; his scream was as sharp as the cold wind. When his breath was gone he lifted his face with teeth clenched and bared.

"Come on, Bob," said Slim, tugging at his shoulder.

"Nigger, you'll freeze to death like that," admonished Al.

"Here," said Jake. "Make 'im drink."

"Hold 'im up! He can't stand!"

"Here, Bob, drink! It'll make you feel better!"

"Hell, he won't drink."

"But, shucks, we got to make 'im drink. How you going to lug 'im home with him moaning and screaming like that?"

Al and Slim lifted Bob, and Jake forced whiskey down his throat.

"Drink, man! You'll catch pneumonia fooling around like this."

The whiskey drooled down Bob's lips and chin.

"Take 'im home," said Jake.

Al and Slim moved forward heavily, supporting Bob between them.

"Well, so long."

"So long."

Jake heard Slim's whacking cough, heard Al's heavy voice pleading with Bob, heard their footsteps crunching in the snow, dying away. He watched them bend against the icy wind as they turned a corner.

He was alone in the deserted street with a deep sense of desolation. He could hardly hold his eyes open. His head throbbed and a loud ringing filled his ears. He pulled his hat low over his face, felt the flask in his hip pocket, patted it, and sneezed. *Hell,* he sighed and wiped his nose with the back of his hand. Whiskey burned like a ball of fire in his solar plexus and braced him against the wind. Each step he took called for concentration and effort. He coughed and a string of phlegm swung from his lips. He bent over and shook; it still swung. He caught the string between his fingers and flung it to the snow. He stumbled blindly as the full force of the alcohol swept over him. Holding to a lamppost, he took out his money and counted it, piece by piece. He had exactly eighty-five cents. *One hundred dollars gone in one night! And I got to pay Doc. Gawddamn that whore!* He straightened, smiled, and yelled to the top of his voice:

"BUT WHEN I WAS FLYING I WAS A FLYING FOOL!"

He tried to put his money back into his pocket and dropped the nickels and dimes into the soft snow. He scratched with his fingers, but could not find a penny. He spat and lurched on. *Shucks, there's more money where that come from.* His mind cleared a bit and he found himself standing on a dark corner. A streetcar clanked by. He looked up, startled. Then he simpered and waved his hand at the car's disappearing tail light. A cold, swift wind lifted his hat and carried it into darkness. He clutched wildly. Stumbled.

"That sonofaBITCH!

He was a block from home now. Just as he was about to step into the street a black limousine shot past and set his coat and tie awry. He wagged his head. *Got to be careful. Can't get run over. Naw, naw, not by a long shot.* He took another drink and things began to whirl. Streetlamps swelled to the size of dull moons, rising and falling when he lowered and lifted his eyes. The snow-covered pavement developed tall hillocks and deep valleys. Hard lines curved sinuously and curves assumed the rigidity of angles. Another streetcar flew by, its screech gritting painfully into his raw nerves. He stopped and shouted:

"WHEN YOU GET TO WHERE YOU GOING TELL 'EM ABOUT ME!"

After what seemed hours of confusion he found himself hugging tightly at a steel telephone pole, opposite his home. A dim light burned in his window. *Yeah, she's up there! I'm going up and pay her off tonight! By Gawd, I'll teach her who's boss, who wears the pants. . . .* When in the vestibule it took him five minutes to find his keys and open the door. He paused several times on the stairs and shook his head to clear away the mists. He listened in front of his flat, but could not hear a sound. The key finally found the hole and he pushed the door in softly. He stood a moment, as though frozen, looking, not breathing. On the edge of a

185

circle of light cast by the floor lamp Lil knelt at the side of the bed, her face lying on the quilt, turned toward him. She was asleep. *Ain't this a bitch! Gone to sleep on her knees, praying. . . . So help me Gawd, I'm going to give her something to pray for!* He slipped off his coat and hat and dropped them to the floor. The room was like a dim, warm dream, and his head seemed far away from his body, whirling. He stuck a cigarette in the corner of his mouth and lit it, then brought out the half-filled flask, still watching Lil sleeping on her knees. He drained the bottle and waited. His flesh began to tingle; a hot flame spread out from his stomach and engulfed him. The room swayed. His lips flexed and he hurled the empty bottle with a swift motion square into the dresser mirror. There was a crash and splintering glass showered the floor. Lil awoke with a violent start and straightened in fright. She screamed and backed into a corner while still on her knees. Jake lurched toward her.

"That wake you up?"

"Jake!"

"Yeeeah, this is Jake. Ain't you glad to see me?"

"You drunk," she breathed.

"How you think I'd be?"

"Please, Jake! You drunk, go to bed!"

"Like hell I will! I'm going to learn you something tonight!"

She was sitting on her knees with her legs doubled under her. He looked at the brown sweep of her calves, brown that dissolved and merged with the warm air of the room.

"Get up!"

"Hush," she whispered. "Folks can hear you."

"GAWDDAMMIT, I WANT 'EM TO HEAR!"

She started to cry.

"You thought you was going to make me lose my job, didn't you? Well, you didn't! I still got it and I'm going to keep it even if I have to split your head wide open!" He was standing over her, his face wet with sweat, his eyes red. "Next time you snitch on me I'm going to send you to the crazyhouse, you hear? The white folks said you was crazy, and you is! You hear me, YOU CRAZY!"

"You'll wake everybody up, Jake. You drunk. . . ."

"GAWDDAMN RIGHT I'M DRUNK! I want the world to know I'm drunk! I don't care what they think! They don't feed me! And I want 'em to know you's a lousy, crazy bitch!"

"Gawd have mercy on you, Jake."

"I don't want nobody to have no mercy on me!"

186

"You don't never stay home and when you do come in you come in drunk."

"What I want to stay home for? To look at *you*? Like hell!"

"While you out having a good time with your money, I'm here sick and hungry."

"That's your hard luck!"

"You got your friends to drink and talk with and I ain't got nothing."

"You don't need nothing."

"Jake, don't you never think of nobody but yourself?"

"Gawd made me like I is, and I'm going to stay that way!"

"You making my life full of misery."

"Look at me! I'm laughing, ain't I?"

"You kill everything you touch."

"If you don't shut your big mouth I *will* kill you!"

He caught the wall to steady himself. His cigarette fell from his lips and hot sparks showered his hands. A hammer of pain beat at the base of his skull. Fumes of darkness circled around him: he was straining with all his might to keep from falling. He kept telling himself, *I got to show her. I got to show this bitch something!* He grabbed the window shade and gave it a twist that sent it to the top of the ceiling, flapping. *I'll show her!* He turned to the dresser and reached three times for a toy glass elephant; finally he caught it in his fist. The room whirled and Lil's brown legs whirled with it, crowding his eyes. He threw the elephant into the windowpane; glass splintered and icy wind rushed in.

"Jake! Jake!"

He threw a bowl. A brush. A glass puppy. He reached for something else; the room tilted and he pulled off the dresser scarf, emptying the things on the floor with a loud clatter. There was a heavy deafness in his ears and he had to shout in order to hear himself.

"LET 'EM HEAR! LET 'EM HEAR!"

He tried to get to her and stumbled over a chair. She rose, crouching, her mouth open, her eyes wide. With numbed fingers he clutched a handful of her gown on each shoulder and jerked.

"Don't beat me! Don't beat me, Jake!"

He grabbed for her throat and she gave a lunge; he went backwards and pulled her with him. She got up and started for the door. While still on his knees he caught the hem of her gown and held her. He stumbled to his feet and rammed her against a wall.

"You hit me, didn't you?"

"Naw, Jake!"

He ripped her gown half open. She sucked her breath in
sharply, lunged again and threw him against the bed. When
she struggled for the door this time he caught her wrist
and swung her around.

"I'm going to see how sick you is!"

She tried to wrench herself free.

"Where you think you going?"

"Naw, naw," she spoke in a breath softer than a whisper
with her eyes fixed in horror upon his face. He attempted
to drag her to the middle of the floor and she sank to her
knees. He tried to lift her and she bit his hand. Blood
leaped to his head and he knocked her into the floor lamp,
sending it sprawling. The room darkened save for the cold
light of the sky.

"You bitch!" he breathed in a voice half curse and half
sob.

He bent and slapped her across her eyes and she
screamed. He bent to slap her again but she eluded him
and crawled over the bed. Her cheeks were bleeding. He
looked at her, his breath coming slowly and heavily through
his open mouth, drying his lips. The room was freezing
cold; in the semidarkness he saw her breath turning white
as it struck the icy wind. *I'm going to fix you!* When he
went toward her she stooped quickly and came up with a
jagged edge of windowpane clutched in her fist. Her voice
was high, hysterical, in one breath, on a dead level.

"Naw. . . . Naw. . . ."

His jaw sagged. He swallowed, wanting another drink.

"Put that glass down!"

He lunged for her arm and missed.

"JAKE!"

When he grabbed for her again she brought the piece of
glass down across his head. A hot anger made him hold
his breath.

"I'm going to kill you!"

She backed to the wall, holding the piece of glass above
her head. He leapt, trying to grasp her wrists; she struck
him again. He staggered, growled, and tried to catch her
hand. When she hit him this time he flopped weakly on the
bed; he felt something warm oozing down his left cheek.
A black whirlpool was sucking him under. He looked
dully at the busted window, at the shards of glass glinting
fitfully on the floor. He dabbed at his scalp with the edge
of a sheet and fumbled at his shirt with sticky fingers,
leaving red prints. He rubbed his eyes and face clumsily
with cold fists and a convulsion of nervous misery made
him sigh out a plaintive whimper. His face twitched. He
belched. He shuddered from the chill that was seeping

188

into the marrow of his bones as darkness roared in his brain.

Lil dropped the piece of glass; its edges were stained from cuts in her hand. She stood over Jake a moment and watched his drunken sleep. Then she pulled down the shade, wrapped herself in a coat and sank to the floor. She pressed a wad of her gown hard into the cuts in her palm to stem the flow of blood and rested her head on her knees.

"Lawd, I wish I was dead," she sobbed softly.

Outside an icy wind swept around the corner of the building, whining and moaning like an idiot in a deep black pit.

Written before *Native Son*, but originally
published several years after Richard Wright's
death in 1960, *Lawd Today* can be seen as a
dark blueprint for the novelist's later works.
It is a characteristically brooding and raw
account—of one day in the life of a Chicago
postal clerk during the Depression. From an
uneasy beginning, the day swerves uncertainly
between despair and exhilaration, and Wright
portrays his protagonist's commotion with
an unerring sense of the jarring rhythms of
experience for the young, the volatile, and
the disaffected.

"The day is described in unsparing detail. . . .
We do come to know not only the society in
which Jake lives, but also, Jake himself, and
despicable as he is, we come to feel with him
and for him."   —*Saturday Review*

"This posthumous book is like the other in
spirit—raw, violent, blasphemous, painfully
direct and honest."   —*Critic*

Cover design by Ann Twombly
Cover illustration by Michael McCurdy

ISBN 0-930350-99-5

Northeastern University Press
Boston, Massachusetts

9 780930 350994

FICTION   Wright, Richard, 1908-1960.
             Lawd Today.

24 ADAMSVILLE - COLLIER HEIGHTS